CLOSING THE GAP BETWEEN RISK AND RESILIENCE

Other Titles by Harriet D. Porton

Teaching the Standards: How to Blend Common Core State Standards into Secondary Instruction (2013)

CLOSING THE GAP BETWEEN RISK AND RESILIENCE

How Struggling Learners Can Cope with the Common Core State Standards

Harriet D. Porton

ROWMAN & LITTLEFIELD EDUCATION

A division of
ROWMAN & LITTLEFIELD
Lanham • Boulder • New York • Toronto • Plymouth, UK

Published by Rowman & Littlefield Education
A division of Rowman & Littlefield
4501 Forbes Boulevard, Suite 200, Lanham, Maryland 20706
www.rowman.com

10 Thornbury Road, Plymouth PL6 7PP, United Kingdom

British Library Cataloguing in Publication Information Available

Library of Congress Cataloging-in-Publication Data Available

ISBN 978-1-4758-0575-8 (cloth : alk. paper)—ISBN 978-1-4758-0576-5 (pbk. : alk. paper)—ISBN 978-1-4758-0577-2 (electronic)

∞™ The paper used in this publication meets the minimum requirements of American National Standard for Information Sciences—Permanence of Paper for Printed Library Materials, ANSI/NISO Z39.48-1992.

Printed in the United States of America

This book is dedicated to the
most important teachers in my life:

IN LOVING MEMORY OF

My first and best teacher, my mom, Rosalie B. Dorfman
My mother-in-law, Bertha Speter, for inspiring me and
teaching me the true meaning of courage and faith

IN GRATITUDE TO

My mentor in everything rigorous,
Dr. Eli Velder

My mentor in everything logical, scientific, and mathematical,
my husband, Stephen Porton

My mentors in everything else, my children,
Debbie Watson and David Schwartz

CONTENTS

PREFACE

> Education is all about building bridges.
>
> —Ralph Ellison

Unless you are teaching only gifted and talented students, someone in your class is likely to be an at-risk learner. Being at risk has almost nothing to do with cognitive skills, but it has everything to do with low school-related self-esteem, an external locus of control, negative schemas about school, and a lack of willingness to take chances while learning. Self-talk among discouraged learners is almost always negative. These students approach learning from an "I don't want to. I can't do it. I don't care" perspective. The advent of Common Core State Standards will not likely be welcomed by this population, and teachers need help closing the gap between their at-risk students and the rigors of the Common Core.

In many respects, this is the book I always wanted to write. Almost every teacher has a story to tell regarding how we knew we were supposed to become teachers. In part, this is mine. When I was little, my sister played piano expertly and spoke French fluently by the time she was in junior high school; my brother earned his PhD in physics from the Johns Hopkins University when he was twenty-one. I could play jacks.

In my family and my culture, mine was not a talent held in high esteem. Nevertheless, I was very lucky. My mom believed that childhood is a time for children to play. She knew that as I grew up, I would find my true calling. Her belief in me began a cycle that has been a part of my life for as long as I can remember. She instilled in me the belief that I could do or be whatever I wanted. I believed in me because she did. If you are reading this book because you love and respect your students, you understand the importance of these convictions.

It wasn't until I started teaching that my real talent became apparent: I can make non-readers devour books. I really can. For example, when my at-risk ninth graders read *The Odyssey*, we learned that "stupid can be fatal." My students discovered that Odysseus never should have told Polyphemus his name, address, and zip code. If he had not done so, his fleet could have come home safely. My students and I had high expectations for each other. My students believed I could teach, and I believed they could learn. When we worked together, failure was never an option.

Common Core State Standards are devoted to bringing rigor and challenging materials to every student. The gap between the goals of the Common Core and the mind-set of struggling learners is obvious and not easily overcome.

This book is devoted to bridging that gap. It is not designed to provide strategies to help general education students who are willing learners succeed with the new standards. It is designed to provide plans, strategies, concepts, and key understandings to educators at the secondary level who teach, supervise, and interact with at-risk learners.

For this book, I suggest all readers pay careful attention to chapters 1–5, as essential skills such as constructing arguments are covered in all these chapters. There are many lesson plans offered for English/language arts. The standards are well elaborated, and this is an area of my expertise. I will never try to write plans for math teachers since they know their content far better than I do. Nevertheless, being an expert in math may put one at a disadvantage when trying to understand students who are terrified by math. The chapter on math offers some insight on the thinking and habits these students display and some suggestions for bridging the gap between the students and math.

It is my hope that those who read this text will have better information, strategies, and ideas for building the bridge between CCSS and struggling learners.

ACKNOWLEDGMENTS

I wish to thank my editor, Tom Koerner, for his support and guidance during my work on this book. He was generous with his time, talent, and patience as I worked from concept to finished manuscript. His assistant, Carlie Wall, has been an important support to me during this process.

In addition, I would like to acknowledge the help I have received on the content of this book. My husband, Steve Porton, reviewed the chapter on math. Barbara Leonard reviewed the chapter on history/social studies. Mary Ann Crimi read the chapters on E/LA. Karen Cifranick helped me with the chapter on science. Everyone needs a peer editor, and I am grateful to all of mine.

I have been blessed with a large and loving family. My family of origin, Bob Dorfman, Susan Levin, and Lucille Karr, are always there to support my efforts. My own children, Debbie Watson and David Schwartz, keep me grounded and happy. My extended family of Jeff and Wendy Porton and Susie and Matt Neuberger has added much joy and richness to my life. In addition, my Duffy clan of Trisha and Mike Swam, Cyndi and Joe Tirone, Bill Duffy, and Tim and Claudia Duffy remind me constantly of what makes a real family. And of course, my writing companion, HRH Lilly R. Porton, is a constant source of unconditional love.

Writing can be a lonely and stressful occupation for me. I could not accomplish my goals without the love and support of my family and friends. I am blessed to have both.

INTRODUCTION

When the rigor of the Common Core State Standards became apparent, it became clear to me that there would be a significant need to build substantive scaffolds between the population most overlooked, struggling learners, and the challenges posed by the Common Core. Unless someone who both knows the nature of at-risk learners and appreciates the many benefits of the CCSS were to provide the support needed, many at-risk students would never even attempt the challenging work the Core requires. It is my goal in this book to close the gap between at-risk learners and the rigors of the CCSS.

The CCSS has encouraged me to tell the stories of my own students' success with rigorous texts. It is possible to make any character relevant to at-risk high school students, and teach informative and narrative texts so well that students continue discussing the work on their way out of class. First, I found that as a teacher you have to find the relevant essential questions embedded in all important works of fiction and non-fiction. Next, you have to be "a guide on the side," not "the sage on the stage" as you and your students discover how to learn life's lessons through reading.

Once you have a clear understanding of the curricular alignments you will have to make, you will be able to make the goals, strategies, and assessments transparent to your students. Think like your students. What do they think they are capable of doing now? Do they believe they have the ability to tackle these new challenges successfully? How do they feel about taking educational risks?

Next, look at what the assessments ask students to do and the strategies and activities you use daily. When the strategies and assessments are aligned well, and you have been successful in developing your students' sense of self-efficacy, you can reach your goals. This text is designed to operationalize these key concepts for all readers.

I think it might be helpful to present the layout of the book to you at this time. First, it is important that all readers share an overview of the current status of CCSS and an introduction to understanding discouraged learners. Next, the text deals with specific informative texts and works of fiction. However, in this unique book, each chapter includes lesson plans that can be used successfully with at-risk learners.

The CCSS in math is almost ready for full implementation. Math teachers know their content, but they are often confused by students' unwillingness to approach any task that involves mathematics. Therefore, the chapter on math provides some insights into the thinking and behavior of math-avoidant students.

The current status of CCSS in science appears to be taking a "go-slow" approach. This is the last of the content areas to be implemented and reliable knowledge is still scarce. Nevertheless, struggling learners will profit from the basic tenets of discovery learning embedded in the new science standards.

In each chapter of the book, reflection exercises are included to help readers process the information provided. It is absolutely necessary, especially when dealing with struggling learners, to be reflective in the planning, implementation, and assessment phases of instruction.

For those of you who believe in yourselves and your students, and who see CCSS as an opportunity to improve your teaching, I have confidence you will find hope and help in my book.

Harriet D. Porton

1

STRUGGLING LEARNERS AND COMMON CORE STATE STANDARDS

Every student can learn, just not on the same day, or the same way.

—George Evans

During the past year, the number of books and chapters written about the Common Core State Standards (CCSS) has increased dramatically. As a result, it has become increasingly clear that students who struggle to learn the current statewide curriculum will require additional support in order to obtain the higher-order thinking skills required by CCSS.

The purpose of this book is to bridge the gap between policy initiatives such as the Common Core and the implementation of these standards when teaching English/language arts, mathematics, social studies, and science to struggling learners.

In this book, struggling learners are defined as follows: (1) students who have an external locus of control; (2) students who are unsuccessful at meeting appropriate grade-level requirements; (3) students who come from marginalized homes and/or communities where the issues at home or in the broader community affect the child's performance in school; and (4) students who have a limited and/or grim notion of the future (Porton, 2013).

IN THIS CHAPTER

The purpose of this chapter is to lay out the history of CCSS, especially in terms of struggling learners. When faced with obstacles as impressive as those faced by struggling learners, it is natural to look into the literature to see what techniques have demonstrated success in the past with this population.

Many teachers have taught struggling learners using cooperative learning strategies and found it to be an effective methodology for teaching and learning. It is an effective system for encouraging peer support, developing connections, and improving work habits.

Since most practitioners want to know how to translate theory into practice, a broad overview of CCSS unit and lesson plans will be provided. Because many struggling learners have displayed a "failure to thrive in school" syndrome, the Habits of Mind procedures for teaching and learning will be reviewed. This model explicitly teaches those skills and behaviors that successful students have internalized and can access easily. Struggling learners, however, are noted for their lack of proficiency with these habits. Finally, an authentic look at differentiation and its utility with this population will be provided.

COMMON CORE STATE STANDARDS

In 1983, when *A Nation at Risk* was released, the government was convinced it had found both the source and the cure for America's poor standing in academic achievement and students' preparation for post–high school success. Over twenty-nine years later, America's schools are still struggling with the same issues. For example, "according to the ACT College Readiness report, 78 percent of high school graduates did not meet the readiness benchmark levels for one or more entry-level college courses in mathematics, science, reading, and English" (Members of the 2005 "Rising above the Gathering Storm" Committee, 2010, p. 11).

The National Governors Association felt so strongly about the depth and breadth of this problem, it worked with the Council of Chief State School Officers to create a common core of state standards. "Common standards that allow us to internationally benchmark our students' performance with other top countries have the potential to bring about a real and meaningful transformation of our education system to the benefit of all Americans" (National Governors Association, 2012, as cited in Common Core State Standards Initiative, p. 1).

Prior to the development of CCSS, American schools functioned under the guidelines set by No Child Left Behind (NCLB). Nevertheless, as long as the standards described and the assessments created as a result of No Child Left Behind only required students to read, recall, and recite, students' ability to create in-depth analyses and interpretations of informative and fictional texts and demonstrate genuine understanding of mathematical principles were unlikely results of standard teaching practices.

During the same time period that the CCSS was being developed, the presidents of the National Academy of Sciences, National Academy of Engineering, and Institute of Medicine were asked to respond to a request made by a bipartisan group of senators and members of Congress and find answers to these questions:

> What are the top 10 actions, in priority order, that federal policymakers could take to enhance the science and technology enterprise so that the United States can successfully compete, prosper, and be secure in the global community of the 21st century? What strategy, with several concrete steps, could be used to implement each of those actions? (Bingaman & Alexander, as cited in *Rising above the Gathering Storm Revisited*, 2010, p. ix)

The concerns that generated this request from Congress mirrored the issues described by the governors and state boards of education, that is, unease about the capacity of America's public schools to provide a rigorous education that will make it possible for the United States to compete in a worldwide global economy. American schools do not inspire confidence in their ability to develop a workforce to support innovative, flexible, and cutting-edge business, medical, and technological advances.

Although the "Gathering Storm" was commissioned by Congress, its previous educational mandate, No Child Left Behind, did not produce many of its stated outcomes. One of the great drawbacks of No Child Left Behind was its failure to provide adequate funding to support schools and school systems as they attempted to make the changes required to meet the stated legislative goals of better educated and more internationally competitive American students.

To avoid that possibility, the Obama administration tied its grant funding initiative Race to the Top to states adopting CCSS. According to a fact sheet prepared by the White House, “backed by a historic $4.35 billion investment, the reforms contained in Race to the Top will help prepare America’s students to graduate ready for college and career, and enable them to out-compete any worker, anywhere in the world” (White House Fact Sheet, 2009, p. 1).

In order to earn all possible points in the Race to the Top grant competition, states needed to sign on to the core standards. As of 2012, forty-five states and three territories have adopted the Common Core State Standards.

Despite its widespread acceptance, CCSS has many obstacles to overcome. As recently as February of 2012, educators across the nation have been frustrated in their attempts to find teaching resources that truly reflect the spirit and the letter of the Core. To make the leap from what some teachers believe their students can do to what the CCSS expects them to accomplish requires further scrutiny.

For example, a principal at a high school in Missouri complained, “There seems to be very little out there, or it’s just not in places we can find it. To say we are prepared for common core would be a misconception” (Gewertz, 2012, p. 1). Perhaps due to the paucity of resources, confusion surrounding CCSS abounds.

According to Rothman (2011), “The Common Core State Standards are one of the most significant initiatives in American education in decades. Yet the swiftness with which they were developed and adopted has left educators uncertain about exactly what they are” (p. 1).

Struggling Learners and Common Core State Standards

Struggling learners and students with learning problems are distinguished for the quantity and quality of scaffolding needed to help them comprehend rigorous texts. For these purposes, an examination of Vygotsky’s seminal work has utility here.

Vygotsky’s theory of the zone of proximal development gives a brilliant description of scaffolding. The zone of proximal development is defined as “the distance between the actual developmental level as determined by independent problem solving and the level of potential development as determined through problem solving under adult guidance, or in collaboration with more capable peers” (Vygotsky, 1978, as cited in McLeod, 2010, p. 1).

When instructors use scaffolding effectively, they introduce new concepts first by providing all the assistance needed directly or by using peer helpers. However, as the learning progresses, the teacher expects students to handle more materials independently.

Another aspect of this theory is that teachers must determine the level of difficulty each student can handle with assistance and measure progress against how much the student learns with decreasing levels of assistance (http://ww35scaffoldingineducation.net). Common Core State Standards clearly embrace the construct of scaffolding as it is mentioned throughout the standards.

Special Problems Faced by At-Risk Students

Throughout the literature on at-risk students, a few principles have become clear. Typically, this population is cynical, filled with a low sense of self-efficacy, diminished self-esteem, and a negative schema about schools, teachers, and their own potential. They do not believe in the connection between effort and achievement. Therefore, they reason, there is no need to try hard in order to reach one's goals because success is considered improbable at best (Porton, 2013; Sagor, 1993).

Despite this negative schema, many at-risk students have become more resilient as a result of teachers who are best described as "warm demanders" (Kleinfeld, 1975), that is, those who hold high expectations for all learners, but who treat every student with respect. In a safe learning environment, where the expectations are clear, high, and consistent, students often learn to trust their teachers and attempt challenging tasks with an enhanced sense of self-efficacy.

High Expectations

Struggling learners may require appropriate modifications and accommodations, but that should not prevent them from being taught in a classroom culture and climate that supports high expectations for all learners. Nevertheless, some of the problems students with disabilities face are the result of their teachers' low expectations.

According to Turnbull (2002), using Universal Design for Learning (UDL), inclusion, collaboration, and multicultural responsiveness, teachers can implement the best practices for meeting the needs of students with IEPs and their non-disabled peers who take classes together. For example, the UDL framework, which CCSS utilizes, explicitly promotes presentation of information in multiple ways and allows for students to express what they have learned in "diverse avenues of action and expression" (Common Core State Standards, 2012).

Current Status of CCSS

Even though there is still crucial information regarding assessments that is not available at the time of this writing, there are steps that teachers should be taking now that will prepare them for CCSS. Current and pre-service teachers should become familiar with the programs and agencies that support it.

Universal Design for Learning is the curricular framework used by CCSS. According to its Fact Sheet No. 2, 2007, "Universal Design for Learning (UDL) is an approach to curriculum design that can help teachers customize curriculum to serve *all* learners" (p. 1). UDL supports multiple forms of instruction, including the following: multiple means of representation so that teachers can use technology, projects, and other formats to help their students learn.

Multiple means of expression allow students to demonstrate their knowledge beyond the traditional paper/pencil type of responses. According to Common Core State Standards, multiple means of engagement means offering students choices, and motivating learners by using authentic strategies that encourage and challenge students to engage in rigorous tasks without undue apprehension.

According to Lewin (2010), the Bill and Melinda Gates Foundation, among many other supporters, has invested in CCSS by underwriting the production of a Literacy Design Collaborative (LDC), which designs templates and rubrics to advance students' success at using the Core. "Modules written by the Literacy Design Collaborative (LDC) are designed to support core-content teachers in implementing the Common Core Standards" (p. 1). Unlike other materials available to practitioners at this time, the LDC are quite robust.

INSTRUCTIONAL CHANGES

Even though CCSS enjoys widespread support, it still presents many challenges to practitioners. Few classroom teachers feel adequately prepared to reformat their individual lesson plans to meet CCSS requirements. Davis (2012) suggests looking at the big picture first, rather than trying to translate each detail described in the standards.

For example, classroom discussions are excellent forums for allowing young adult learners to analyze an issue from a position that is in direct opposition to their own. In addition, teachers using classroom discussions as a methodology can teach students how to listen to learn, not just wait for their turn to talk, and use evidence-based data, not emotional appeal, to support their stands.

There is valuable material available (Barton, Heilker, & Rutkowski, 1997; Porton, 2013) which provides explicit suggestions for conducting effective classroom discussions that help students move from "I think" based on weak anecdotal evidence to "credible research in this field indicates" based on research skills developed in multiple small research projects. Unlike the current statewide assessments that only measure memory, CCSS assessments will measure students' understanding of mathematical principles and the underlying connotations and denotations of rigorous texts.

Teachers do not like to waste their time, and neither do students. Writing to real audiences rather than "another student in another school or a fictitious character" can encourage even reluctant writers to write for a real purpose in order to develop and expand their understanding of important issues. For example, if one lives in Maryland, and Dr. Ben Carson, a renowned neurosurgeon, was on the medical staff at Johns Hopkins Hospital, based on a related reading, it makes sense to ask a student who is interested in science to write and send a letter regarding a legitimate medical question to Dr. Carson.

CCSS is very clear about the importance of teaching argument and the rules of evidence that apply, rather than persuasion, which only requires writers and speakers to voice opinions. There are several sources available on this topic. Hillocks' (2011) text *Teaching Argument and Writing Grades 6–12* provides a hierarchy of teaching students how to frame arguments from basic to complex topics. Using Toulmin's seminal work on claim-evidence-warrants by going to home.comcast.net/cphenlymbk2006/IBMA/claim-evidence-warrant[1].pdf, teachers can find definitions and examples that can be used now to help their students learn how to write and speak insightfully about topics that are currently in dispute.

The Appendices for the Common Core State Standards is an excellent resource for getting a more thorough picture of how CCSS evaluates text complexity. No longer satisfied with the past flawed systems for determining readability, the new system accurately acknowledges that reading is much more complex than sentence length and the number of syllables in words in a selected passage would indicate. Even mildly cognitively impaired students push through complex texts if the topic is of interest to them, the format engaging and familiar, and the end result perceived to be worthwhile.

COOPERATIVE LEARNING

Nevertheless, despite the issues that create the gap between CCSS expectations and struggling learners, some procedures have proven to be very successful with our target audience. The use of cooperative learning provides credible data for implementing its use in any classroom, but especially in programs for at-risk youth.

According to Johnson and Johnson (2009), cooperative learning's success can be traced to the relationships among theory, research, and practice. As leading experts in the field, Johnson and Johnson have a vested interest in its success; however, other researchers in different countries have validated its utility.

For example, Gillies (2008), reviewing the effects of cooperative learning in Australia, found that students who participated in cooperative learning showed more complex thinking and sophisticated problem-solving skills than their peers. In addition, "Cooperative learning is of value for all students including those who have been identified as 'at risk,' 'bilingual,' 'gifted,' and 'normal.' All students need to learn and work in environments where their individual strengths are recognized and individual needs are addressed. All students need to learn within a supportive community in order to feel safe enough to take risks" (Sapon-Shevin, Ayers, & Duncan, 1994, p. 2).

The Coleman Report (1966) on the efficacy of the millions of dollars spent as a result of Johnson's War on Poverty and the 1964 Civil

Rights Act reviewed all of the interventions to determine which, if any, had any statistically significant impact on students' success as a result of the government's input. According to the analyses, three variables were found to have a positive effect on the results: (1) female teachers' SAT scores in math, (2) values held by the students' families, and (3) the integration of minority students into mostly white schools.

Although there is hotly contested debate on these findings, the importance of a secure environment for developing students' potential is not in question. Therefore, the duplication of a functional family unit in the form of teams that require every member to be responsible, loyal, and committed to mutual success may be accomplished in school through the use of cooperative learning (Porton, 2013).

Creating Effective Teams

In an effective team, each student knows what is expected, works for the benefit of the team, develops a sense of loyalty to his/her team, and takes personal responsibility for his/her work.

Team Roles:

1 = Team leader
Keeps team on task.
2 = Team recorder
Takes notes during team discussions.
3 = Materials person
Gets materials for team.
4 = Team spokesperson
Answers team questions for the team.

A simple procedure for creating cooperative learning teams is easy to follow. Number One person, the team leader, always has an excellent work ethic and high status among his/her peers. Number Two has good attendance and adequate writing skills, as that person is the recorder for the group. Number Three has a less reliable work ethic but can be encouraged to do the work if the team leader is strong. This person gets all the needed supplies for the team. Number Four person has the least functional work ethic. This is the team's spokesperson who answers all questions on behalf of the team. This person can always call for a "team

Figure 1.1.

time out" if he/she needs additional clarification from the team. In order to accomplish a lot of the team's work, the use of placemats is highly recommended. (See figure 1.2.)

In the empty square at the center of the placemat, teachers place an extra point if all of the team's members are present in school that day, if every member of the team is on task, and if all supplies needed for the day's lesson are on each student's desk.

Each student places his/her answer to the warm-up in the spot designated by the student's team number. Using this process, students are grouped on work ethic, rather than ability. Work ethic is the variable that makes the most difference between students' success and failure. This is especially true when working with struggling learners. Ability is a function of both natural intellectual strengths and adaptability.

The Placemat

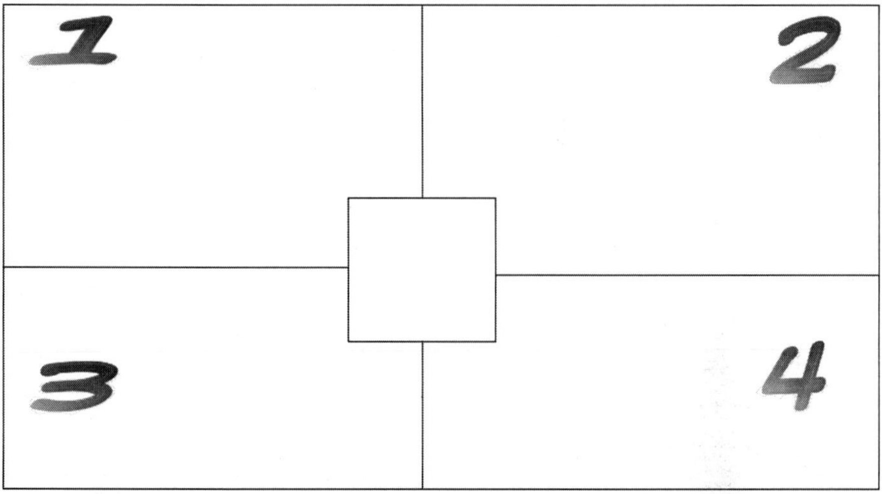

Figure 1.2.

According to Sternberg, intelligence is best shown in unexpected circumstances that challenge a person's ability to deal with the environment to which he/she must adapt (in Kaufman & Grigorenko, 2008). However, successful work habits can be taught, can impact anyone's success, can be very meaningful, and can be improved with effective instructional strategies, for example, Habits of Mind.

> There is growing interest in the role of a dispositional construct developed by Lounsbury et al. (2003) that appears to be predictive of academic and job performance-work drive: "an enduring motivation to expend time and effort to finish projects, meet deadlines, be productive, and achieve success" (Lounsbury & Gibson, 2002; Lounsbury, Sundstrom, Loveland, & Gibson, 2003). Rau and Durand (2000) studied a similar construct, academic ethic, and also found that it predicted college grades. (Ridgell & Lounsbury, 2004, p. 1)

If work ethic can be predictive of college success with non-impaired students, it can be a powerful predictor of success when students have access to appropriate modifications, accommodations, and differentiated learning experiences. This is one reason why work ethic is the best variable to use for grouping students in teams.

In addition, using a protocol shared with Harford County Public School teachers by inclusion teachers at Thomas Jefferson High School in Frederick County, Maryland, Harford County teachers found that the use of senior tutors was a key facet of success with students in cooperative-collaborative classes. At the end of each school year, general education inclusion teachers went into junior English classes, except AP or Gifted and Talented 11, to recruit senior tutors for their inclusion classes.

The seniors received a grade for their work in the inclusion class. They were expected to work with their assigned teams, help individuals who needed extra support, and keep their teams on task. Their failure to do so resulted in a poor grade and dismissal from the program. I am not aware of any data collected on this practice, but I know from personal experience that both the seniors' and their freshmen's skills grew exponentially as a result of this experience.

Note:

Recently I field-tested a Habits of Mind lesson with an excellent special educator, Ms. Hall, at a working-class, mixed-demographic middle school. Working the way that experienced and respectful general and special educators can work, we implemented this lesson successfully. Ms. Hall had created modified forms of the warm-up and assessment for her students even before I arrived. When I came home from teaching the lesson, with her permission I added them to my plan. I also added the handout on team roles to the original plan. It has special utility when you start using cooperative learning, and for a "traveling salesperson" like me, it is essential.

The students in this class were extraordinarily polite and receptive, but they had trouble remembering their numbers and what their numbers meant. Therefore, when I got home that day, I made five sets of index cards to take with me to every class I visited from then on so that the students would have their numbers and the job associated in front of them all the time. When I was a classroom teacher, these were laminated and placed on every student's desk until the routines were internalized, but I had not thought of making them portable before this teaching experience.

In addition, during this and my other field-testing events, I did not see a need for extra motivational activities beyond my normal "review for prior students' knowledge" or "how will this lesson apply to you?" techniques. I believe that if the topic is meaningful and the students believe the teacher will provide adequate scaffolding, additional and/or more intensive motivational strategies do not appear to be needed.

HABITS OF MIND

One of the deeply held beliefs that are at the heart of pedagogical teaching and practices is that goals, strategies, and assessments must be aligned and transparent in every lesson. When that is true, students' academic growth improves, especially when they know what they are learning, how they are learning, and how they will be assessed. To clarify these relationships, the Instructional Triangle (figure 1.3) was created (Porton, 2013).

One of the principal ideas articulated throughout the CCSS is that students must be required to remain focused and persevere while working with challenging texts in order to master rigorous content. "Through wide and deep reading of literature and literary nonfiction of steadily increasing sophistication, students gain a reservoir of literary and cultural knowledge, references, and images; the ability to evaluate intricate arguments; and the capacity to surmount the challenges posed by complex texts" (www.corestandards.org/the-standards/).

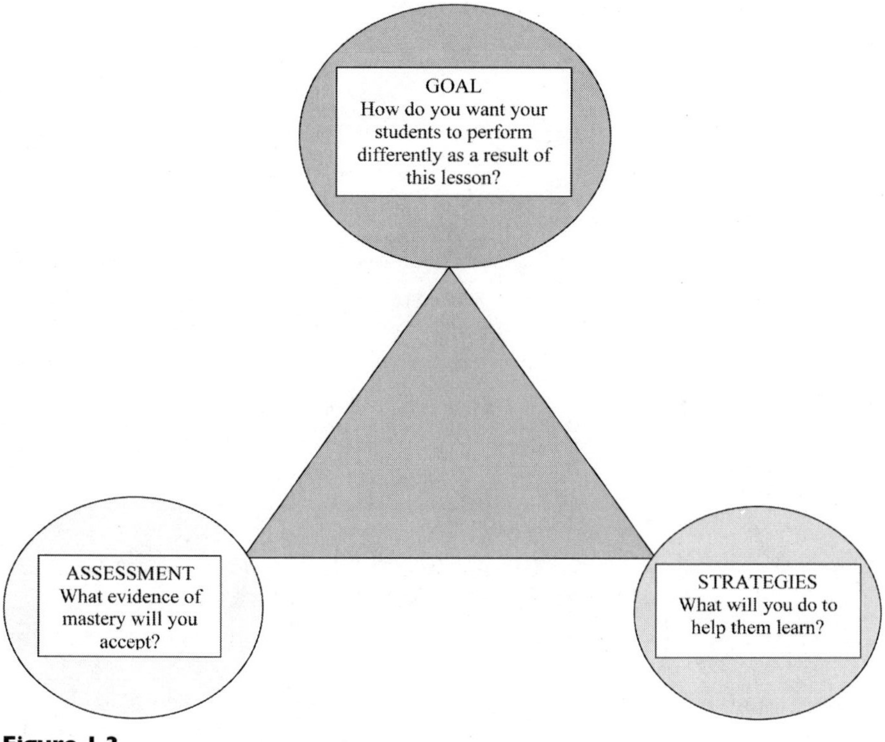

Figure 1.3.

Many high school teachers expect their students to have mastered the following attributes before ninth grade. However, there is usually a gap between what teachers want their students to be able to do and the reality that faces educators each day. Using Campbell's (2006) model can help to clarify those behaviors that specifically lead to effective Habits of Mind behaviors.

At least one of the Habits of Mind described in table 1.1 should be reflected in every lesson plan's goals, strategies, and assessments relative to the students' content, and the material being covered. Once teachers have reviewed the day's Habits of Mind goal, they must explain its meaning, describe associated behaviors, model, and then reinforce its use. However, if there is no assessment that measures students' proficiency, it will not be valued by high school students. Secondary students believe in the relative importance of any skill based on whether or not they are held accountable for its use.

Table 1.1.

Habits of Mind	*Description*
Persisting	Persevering in a task through completion. Not giving up.
Managing impulsivity	Taking time to deliberate before acting.
Listening with understanding and empathy	Making the effort to perceive another person's perspective.
Thinking flexibly	Considering options and changing perspectives.
Metacognition	Thinking about your thinking. Being aware of your thoughts, feelings, and actions, and their effects on others.
Striving for accuracy	Setting high standards and finding ways to improve.
Questioning and problem solving	Finding problems to solve. Seeking data and answers.
Applying past knowledge to new situations	Accessing prior knowledge and transferring this knowledge to new contexts.
Thinking and communicating with clarity and precision	Striving for accurate oral and written communication.
Taking responsible risks	Living on the edge of one's competence.
Thinking interdependently	Being able to work and learn with others in teams.
Remaining open to continuous learning	Resisting complacency in learning and admitting when one does not know.

In order to be sure that students know how to demonstrate any of the Habits of Mind, teachers can use a brief focus lesson to help students practice any targeted skill they are having difficulty acquiring. The following (table 1.2) is a problem-solving scenario that requires students to think interdependently, listen with empathy, apply past knowledge, and be creative, imaginative, and inventive. However, persistence is the Habits of Mind skill which is considered most important in this lesson. The point value for each question reflects the emphasis placed on this skill.

The purpose of using a focus lesson is to give students an opportunity to internalize an important Habit of the Mind skill without any concerns regarding content. However, once teachers have practiced the newly acquired skill, they can begin to expect their students to demonstrate the targeted skill with enhanced aptitude in order to improve their overall academic performance.

DIFFERENTIATION

Carol Ann Tomlinson, the acknowledged expert on differentiation, has provided a framework for understanding the promise in the practice of differentiation. Nowhere does that procedure have more utility than when teachers bridge the gap between CCSS and struggling learners.

According to Tomlinson and Strickland (2005) the United States is moving to a more culturally diverse nation of minorities. In order to reach the diverse population of students who attend American schools, "schools will have to move from standardized instruction to personalized instruction" (p. 1). Due to CCSS, all students, rather than just the elite highly advanced learners, will have to learn problem solving and higher-order and flexible thinking skills and become capable producers, not just consumers of knowledge.

Tomlinson and Strickland (2005) provide a great deal of supporting data that validates their claims. "Theodore Sizer (1992) reminds us that while it may be inconvenient that students differ, it is an irrefutable fact of life in the classroom" (p. 2).

Sizer, 1992 (as cited in Tomlinson & Strickland, 2005) argues that if schools want students to become productive, reach high standards, and utilize higher-order thinking skills, students' diversity should be

Table 1.2. Content-Free Lesson Plan

Habits of Mind Objective	As a result of participating in this lesson, each student will demonstrate the ability to persist until the entire problem has been solved.
Warm up	On your own paper, answer the following questions: Have you ever been at work or home when disaster struck, and you had to figure out how to solve the problems? How did you feel? What did you do? What happened? Discuss your responses with the team.
Guided Practice	In this lesson, we will be working on *persistence*. As a class, we will discuss behaviors connected to persistence. Each team will be given the same scenario and asked to resolve the same problems. Grades will be determined for teams by the responses each team provides. Individuals will earn points based on each student's efforts to stay on task until the entire problem is solved. What should she do? Tonya is working at the restaurant, and the manager calls to say she cannot come to work and will not be available. A few minutes later, one of her coworkers calls to say he was in a car accident and will not be able to come to work. Tonya and one other person are left alone to deal with the dinner rush. As a team, tell Tonya how to handle the following situations: 1. The deep-fat fryer is making strange noises. 2. A group of kids comes in, and they harass other customers. 3. Tonya's coworker gets into an argument with a customer. 4. The safe is locked, and she does not have the combination (manager is *not* available). Model problem: Tonya's best friend comes in and asks for free food. The friend really has no money, but everyone is watching Tonya.
Independent Practice	Each team must create answers to the above questions (1–4) and justify their decisions in writing. These guidelines must be followed: 1. Tonya cannot leave work. 2. All problems must be solved appropriately. 3. Outside resources can be used, but only after trying to solve the problem alone. 4. One *creative* solution is provided for one of the problems.
Assessment 90 points	10 points for each good answer 15 points for the creative, innovative answer 45 points for each student who consistently works with the team to create thoughtful, credible, and ingenious answers. • 10—making suggestions/providing alternative solutions/accepting feedback • 10—finding relevant data to support team's decisions • 10—looking for solutions beyond the obvious that could work • 15—persisting even when task/team/situation becomes difficult

embraced, not ignored. In their work on diversity, Tomlinson and Strickland (2005) have operationalized theory into useful suggestions for practice.

For example, when teachers want to differentiate for content in terms of readiness, they are asked to "provide supplementary materials at varied reading levels . . . provide organizers to guide note-taking . . . use videotapes to supplement and support explanations and lectures" (p. 9).

When differentiating for process, teachers are asked to "allow multiple options for how students express learning . . . balance competitive, collegial, and independent work arrangements . . . develop activities that seek multiple perspectives on topics and issues" (p. 10).

E/LA UNIT COMPONENTS AND LESSON PLANS

There will not be a curriculum guide available when CCSS is fully implemented in E/LA and mathematics in 2014; however, each state has been given permission to develop templates for unit plans and lesson plans to help teachers make the necessary transitions. The following template (table 1.3) is the result of the work of a team of writers selected by the Maryland State Department of Education to write grade-level units and specific lesson plans during the late spring of 2012.

It is always better to think about possible obstacles and account for them early in the planning phase than to have to fix unforeseen problems on the back end (B. Malen, personal communications). Therefore, backward mapping before the unit begins is a highly effective tool to be sure that the unit can succeed.

Using the UDL curriculum format requires teachers to have a fully developed conceptual framework for all major units of study. Struggling learners normally are more successful in a planned, orderly, and focused environment.

This planning model offers students a transparent view of their teachers' educational goals, strategies, and assessments. Educators need to promote openness and transparency in order to improve students' trust in faculty members and the assessment process.

Lesson Plans

The Maryland State Department of Education writing team developed a lesson plan format which it believes will help teachers to include all of the CCSS required components.

Table 1.3. E/LA Unit Components

Grade ______
Length of Unit ____________
Unit Title ____________________
Unit Writers ____
(This material will be available to all teachers in Maryland in the fall of 2013, and the authors of the plans posted on the website will be acknowledged).

Unit Overview

Write a brief description of the unit, including the following:
• Controlling idea or central topic
• Rationale—why
• Purpose—what
• Structure—how
  ° Flow of instruction
  ° Student performance

Essential Question
What essential question are students trying to answer as a result of participating in this unit?
Unit Standards
Reading Informational Text Determine which CCSS R. I. strands will be used during the unit and list them here.
Writing Determine which CCSS W. strands will be used during this unit and list them here.
Speaking and Listening Determine which CCSS S. L. strands will be used during this unit and list them here.
Language Determine which CCSS L. strands will be used during this unit and list them here.
Reading for Literature Determine which CCSS R. L. strands will be used during this unit and list them here.

Student Outcomes
In this unit, students will
Suggested Texts
Create a list of all possible informative and fictional texts that can be used during the unit.
Assessments
Pre-assessment: Lesson specific Formative Assessments: discussions, exit tickets, journals

Summative Assessment: End of unit culminating activity (e.g., researched-based project) which demonstrates students' mastery of identified targets.
Lesson Plans

• Differentiation
• UDL
• Essential question
• Standards and strands
• Student outcomes
• Activity procedures
  • Pre-, formative assessments
  • Suggested texts, materials
  • Optional components (by lesson)
    ° Essential background knowledge
    ° Additional resources

Lesson Seeds
The lesson seeds are ideas for the standard that can be used to build a lesson. Lesson seeds are not meant to be all-inclusive, nor are they substitutes for instruction.
Interdisciplinary connections
• History • Mathematics • Science • Music • Art

(Maryland State Department of Education, 2012)

This lesson plan format allows flexibility in the degree of specificity used when planning the procedures for each lesson. However, one of the goals of CCSS is to ensure that any student in a state participating in CCSS gets the same level of rigor, grade-level content, and thorough planning on the part of his/her teacher, no matter where the student lives.

This is another CCSS lesson plan format (table 1.5) which teachers might find useful. It provides an extra component, Habits of Mind target, which teaches and assesses students' growth on the targeted skill.

Literacy Design Collaborative

Fortunately, many benefactors have come to the aid of the educational community to lend their financial support to making CCSS accessible to all teachers. The Bill and Melinda Gates Foundation has been very instrumental in creating templates that classroom teachers can use

Table 1.4.

Lesson Overview
Include • Approximate time of lesson (express as a single day or multiple days) • Summary of lesson, including purpose of lesson, text or media, brief explanation of instructional process, and student products
Teacher Planning and Preparation
Consider • Range of learners and needs for modifications/accommodations/differentiation/struggling learners • Pre-reading of texts and rehearsal of delivery • Assembling appropriate numbers of written text and other media • Preparation for grouping options • Creation of PowerPoint presentation/organizers/assessments
Essential Question
What question are the students trying to answer as a result of participating in today's lesson as it relates to the whole unit?
Unit Standards Applicable to This Lesson
• List standard for reading literature and/or informative texts • List writing standards • List speaking and listening standards • List language standards
Student Outcomes
List those skills/knowledge/processes the students will master as a result of participating in today's lesson.
Materials
• List the materials all students will need in order to participate in this lesson. • List the modifications/accommodations which students with disabilities are entitled to in today's class.
Pre-assessment
• Pre-assess to discover the presence or absence of required background knowledge. • Pre-assess to determine students' skills on specific language targets.
Lesson Procedures
Each teacher needs to create a list of procedures that fits his/her professional style. Some teachers write detailed lists, including questions they will ask, and others use less elaborate lists. Pre-service teachers and teachers who are new to teaching inclusion should write very specific procedural lists.
Lesson Closure
Bring students back to the Essential Question and review their progress as a result of participating in today's lesson.

(Maryland State Department of Education, 2012)

Table 1.5. Lesson Planning Template

Lesson Title
Lesson Unit

Lesson Overview	Purpose of lesson Essential Question
Student Outcomes	As a result of participating in today's lesson, students will . . .
Academic Lesson CCSS Targets for Instruction	Reading Writing Speaking and Listening Language
Habits of Mind Target	Teacher selects the appropriate Habits of Mind skill for this lesson.
Materials Needed	Supplies needed for all students Accommodations/modified materials needed by students with disabilities
Warm up Time	Pre-assessments are used here.
Motivation Time	Discuss key ideas and relate them to students' lives, interests, challenges, experiences, etc.
Guided Practice Time	Teachers introduce and model new learning. Scaffolding involves a lot of teacher support here. Habits of Mind skills are modeled.
Independent Practice Time	At this phase of instruction, close support from the teacher is decreased and students work independently to reach the day's CCSS and Habits of Mind targets.
Assessment Time	Using multiple platforms, students demonstrate their growth in understanding as a result of participating in the day 's lesson.
Habits of Mind	Evaluating the process of acquiring the targeted Habit of Mind, teachers use informal assessments to measure students' progress.
Closure Time	Class returns to the Essential Question and reviews the students' progress at answering the segment of the question covered in the day's class.
Homework	Students practice one of the targeted skills covered in class in a way that is both interesting and meaningful.

to implement the CCSS. "Each module focuses on a specific teaching task and includes the skills students need to be successful, a set of mini-tasks to guide instruction, and a scoring guide or rubric to help assess the students' rate of success" (Anatomy of an LDC Module, 2010, p. 1).

Many of the writing lesson-plan templates offered in this text will include a model of a writing prompt, a generic rubric, and suggestions for student products. For example, "[Insert Essential Question]. After reading ________________ (literature or informational texts), write a/an____________ (essay, report, or substitute) that addresses the question, and support your position with evidence from the text(s). Be sure to acknowledge competing views" (Anatomy of an LDC Module, 2010, p. 1). Since teachers select their reading materials and choose their students' products based on the writing and language strands selected, they will be able to modify any plan using this approach.

POINTS TO PONDER

It is helpful to view the forthcoming CCSS through the lens of its burdens and benefits. When effective lesson planning is studied, it is easy to understand why using the Instructional Triangle, which helps to determine the alignment among goals, strategies, and assessments, is important. In addition, if CCSS requires teachers to use rigorous texts, but the teacher gives his/her students watered-down "high interest, low readability" materials during the strategies section of the lesson, very few, if any, students in the class will be successful at interpreting and responding to challenging texts.

Cooperative learning has demonstrated its effectiveness in multiple settings over many years. One study demonstrated its specific utility with struggling learners. "Low achieving students tend to work harder when grouped with higher achieving students" (Dahey, 2012, p. 2).

Those who wrote the CCSS and current state-level curriculum writers have provided a roadmap, but not a statewide, mandated curriculum guide for teachers to follow. Once again teachers have autonomy, and they are free to make standards attainable for all their students. Popularized by Marzano (1992), the Habits of Mind skills and attributes provide authentic, intentional learning experiences to help students with cognitive and psychosocial impairments duplicate the behaviors common among successful students.

Despite its many benefits, CCSS presents substantive burdens. At the current time, state curriculum writers are designing units, lesson plans, and lesson seeds without having seen the final prototypes of the assessments which will be used to measure students' progress. Habits of Mind skills are not clearly linked into CCSS despite their utility in helping students who are cognitively compromised and struggling learners mimic successful students' behaviors, roles, and skills.

Nevertheless, this chapter has demonstrated that there is a path between what is known about CCSS and teachers' current work with students who are struggling learners. By developing the appropriate scaffolding, by planning intentional differentiation into every lesson, by using cooperative learning, and by creating specific focus lessons for new Habit of Mind skills, teachers can enjoy the benefits and limit the burdens of the challenges posed by the Common Core of State Standards.

REFLECTIONS

There is a substantive gap between what struggling learners are willing to do and what the CCSS expects of them. This gap can be bridged with the appropriate scaffolding, careful lesson planning, and sensitive implementation. All of these require time, patience, and effort. By yourself or with a partner, respond to the following:

1. How does CCSS hope to improve the learning experiences of all students?
2. How will the implementation of CCSS affect instruction in your content area?
3. Create four teams for one of your classes based on their work ethic. What challenges did you encounter?
4. Differentiate the strategies and assessments for a lesson plan you are planning to teach next week. What challenges did you encounter?
5. Keep track of your results after one week of using CCSS-based plans. What do you expect to see? What were the results?

REFERENCES

Barton, J., Heilker, P., & Rutkowski, D. (1997). *Fostering effective classroom discussions.* www.mhhe.com/socscience/english/tc/discussion.htm.

Campbell, J. (2006). *Theorizing habits of mind as a framework for learning.* Grand Queensland University. aasaquinto.2012.pbworks.com.

Coleman, J. S. (1966). Equality of educational opportunity (summary report). U.S. Department of Health, Education, and Welfare, Office of Education.

Common Core State Standards Initiative (2012). www.corestandards.org.

Dahey, A. M. (2012). Cooperative learning classroom research. http://alumni.media.mit.edu/-andyd/mindset/design/ele_rsch.html.

Davis, L. (2012). 5 things every teacher should be doing to meet the Common Core State Standards, Eye of Education, www.eyeoneducation.com.

Gates, Bill & Melinda Foundation. (2010). Anatomy of an LDC Module.

Gerwitz, C. (2012). Educators in search of common-core resources. *Education Week.* www.edweek.org/ew/articles/2012/02/24/22resources_ep.h31.html?tkn=LTOFTpkW.

Gillies, R. W. (2008). The effects of cooperative learning on junior high school students' behaviours, discourse, and learning during a science-based learning activity. *School Psychology International.* Spi.sagepub.com.doi:10.1177/0143034308093673.

Hillocks, G. (1995). *Teaching writing as reflective practice.* New York: Teachers College Press.

Hillocks, G. Jr. (2011). *Teaching argument and writing grades 6–12.* Portsmouth, NH: Heinemann.

Johnson, D. W., & Johnson, R. T. (2009). An educational psychology success story: Social interdependence theory and cooperative learning. *Educational Researcher, 38*(5), 365–379.

Kleinfeld, J. (1975). Effective teachers of Eskimo and Indian Students. *The School Review, 83*(2), 301–344.

Lewin, T. (2010). College see 16% increase in study of sign language. *New York Times.*

Maryland State Department of Education (2012). http://mdk12.org/share/frameworks/CCSS_Reading_Literature_gr6-8.pdf.

Marzano, R. J. (1992). *A different kind of classroom: Teaching with dimensions of Learning.* Association for Supervision and Curriculum Development, 1250 North Pitt Street, Alexandria, VA 22314.

McLeod, S. (2010). www.simplypsychology.org/Zone-of-Proximal-Development.html.

Members of the 2005 "Rising above the Gathering Storm" Committee (2005). *Rising above the gathering storm.* Washington, DC: The National Academic Press.

Porton, H. D. (2013). *Helping struggling students succeed in school.* Boston: Pearson.

Ridgell, S. D., & Lounsbury, J. W. (2004). Predicting academic success: General intelligences, "big five" personality traits, and work drive. *College Student Journal.*

Rothman, R. (2011). Five myths about the common core state standards. *Something in Common, 27*(5), September/October 2011.

Sagor, R. (1993). *At-risk students: Reaching and teaching them.* Swampscott, MA: Watersun Publishing.

Sapon-Shevin, M. B., J. J., Ayres, B. J., & Duncan, J. (1994). Cooperative learning and inclusion. *Creativity and collaborative learning: A practical guide to empowering students and teachers*, 45–58.

Sternberg, R. J., Kaufman, J. C., & Grigorenko, E. (2008). *Applied intelligence.* Cambridge: Cambridge University Press.

Tomlinson, C. A. (2003). *Fulfilling the promise of the Differentiated Classroom.* Alexandria, VA: ASCD.

Tomlinson, C. A., & Strickland, C. A. (2005). *Differentiation in practice: A resource guide for differentiating curriculum grades 9–12.* Alexandria, VA: ASCD.

Turnbull, R. (2002). *Research, teaching, and all that jazz.*

Universal Design for Learning (2007). Professional development: Fact sheet no. 2. American Institute for Research.

The White House, Office of the Press Secretary (2009). Fact sheet: The race to the top. www.whitehouse.gov/the-press-office/fact-sheet-race-top.

2

HOW DOES A JUST PERSON MAKE DECISIONS IN AN UNJUST WORLD?

The sad duty of politics is to establish justice in a sinful world.

—President Jimmy Carter

Adolescents sit on the precipice between childhood and adulthood. To help them understand the difference, I altered Dr. Phil's quote on the difference between losers and winners. I taught my students that "adults do what they have to do; children do what they want to do," explaining that when they do what they have to, they are living up to their responsibilities. When they make decisions based on the greater good rather than their own immediate and personal gratification, they are adults no matter how old they are.

Moral reasoning and making effective decisions about justice are essential components of this paradigm. Injustice is a part of many students' worlds, and it is part of the educational imperative that teachers help children relinquish their primitive moral reasoning and view the world with a sense of both awe and cynicism. They need to understand what a New England abolitionist said long ago: "The moral arc of the universe bends at the elbow of justice" (Parker, 1853, as cited in Stiehm, 2010).

Gay/lesbian rights, the Supreme Court ruling that determined that obtaining an arrestee's DNA is legal under the Fourth Amendment, and President Obama's stand regarding no longer deporting most illegal immigrants who were young children when their parents came to the United States are polarizing topics.

As young adolescents begin to make moral decisions regarding these and similar issues, it is appropriate for them to examine complex issues in a safe and controlled environment. Therefore, the first Essential Question could be as follows: How does a just person make decisions in an unjust world?

As educators of adolescents, teachers need to examine how and where youngsters can acquire the decision-making skills regarding justice and morality that will generalize from their classrooms to their neighborhoods. Cauffman and Steinberg (2009) found that people who demonstrate higher levels of responsibility, perspective, and temperance showed more effective decision-making skills than those who scored lower on these psychosocial factors, regardless of age. Educators must play a part in how and where children learn to acquire these essential skills.

Teachers need to recognize and accept that much of this work has fallen on the shoulders of educators. This is not entirely unreasonable. As James Baldwin said, "For these are all our children, we will all profit by or pay for what they become."

Emotions and culture play a key role in decisions surrounding justice. For example, Immordino-Yang and Demassion (2007) used findings from neuroscience to examine questions related to feeling and thinking. "According to their research, recent advances in neuroscience highlight the correlation between emotion, social functioning and decision making that have the potential to revolutionize our understanding of the role of affect in education.

In particular, the neurobiological evidence suggests that the aspects of cognition that we recruit most heavily in schools, namely learning, attention, memory, decision making, and social functioning are both profoundly affected by, and subsumed within the process of emotion; we call these aspects *emotional thought*" (abstract). They further contend that connections between decision making, moral reasoning, and social functioning may help us to understand the relationships between learning and emotion, how culture shapes learning "and ultimately the development of morality and human ethics" (p. 3). Teachers, therefore, must remember that "emotions that play out in the body and mind are profoundly intertwined with thought" (p. 3).

Therefore, examining questions of morality with adolescents recognizes where they are on their cognitive and affective developmental trajectory. According to a study by Fehr, Rützler, and Sutter (2011), how people regard and treat others develops with age. It appears from their study that spitefulness can decrease with age and egalitarian behaviors can increase. However, none of this development can occur unless children learn the difference between the two. Important and relevant texts can provide youngsters with the opportunity to try out their moral reasoning and learn from their peers, and their teachers.

It is up to teachers to recognize the emotional underpinnings that affect all learners.

On a Personal Note

When I taught a focus lesson regarding Elie Wiesel's acceptance speech for the Nobel Prize to an all-female group of high school students, I told my mother-in-law's story of her life in the Bergen-Belsen Concentration Camp. The girls' evaluations of the lesson indicated that they thought they would remember the lesson longer because they recognized and empathized with my strong feelings.

There is a neurological explanation for this effect. According to Hu et al. (2007), neuroscientists have found that in order to transfer information from short-term into long-term memory, the hippocampus is aided by the emotional load of any experience. Although neuroscientists are still struggling to understand how emotion regulates memory, for these purposes, it is important to recognize that emotion does not interfere with learning; it is a critical component of both learning and memory.

IN THIS CHAPTER

In this chapter, the reading goals come from Reading Information Texts, CCSS Grade 9—Strand—Key Ideas and Details, R.9–10.2: "Determine a central idea of a text and analyze its development over the course of the text, including how it emerges and is shaped and refined by specific details" (CCSS). The informative text is "Letter from Birmingham Jail" by Dr. Martin Luther King (1963). English teachers will examine this nonfiction work through a literary lens. The Habit of the Mind goal for this section is "Thinking flexibly . . . being able to change perspectives, generate alternatives, consider options" (Costa & Kallick, 2009, p. x).

The writing component of this Essential Question will be writing arguments—W.9–10.1.a: "Introduce precise claims, distinguish the claims from alternate or opposing claims, and create an organization that establishes clear relationships among claims, counterclaims, reasons, and evidence" (CCSS). The Habit of the Mind goal for the writing component is "Persisting. Stick to it! Persevering in a task through completion; remaining focused; looking for ways to reach your goal when stuck; not giving up" (Costa & Kallick, 2009, p. x).

However, before the formal discussion begins, it is important to review rhetoric and discuss an outstanding model for teaching students how to improve their writing skills (Killgallon & Killgallon, 2007). Successful writing programs that actually translate process into practice are very rare; these materials are highly recommended.

If teachers use all of the scaffolding necessary, draw on the students' prior knowledge, and use meaningful and appropriate motivational exercises, even their struggling students should reach the standards set by CCSS as well as improve their ability to use their feelings and thinking to recognize successful strategies for making just decisions in an unjust world.

Rhetoric

Rhetoric refers to the idea that even intelligent and well-educated people can and do disagree about hotly contested topics. Rhetoric provides both parties with a formula for discussing disagreements in a healthy and productive manner.

Usually when two people or groups of people disagree it is because they make different assumptions about the topic at hand. Effective arguments are based on recognizing the basic assumptions being made, recognizing the assumptions made by the alternate view, and providing sufficient evidence and warrants to help demonstrate the validity of the argument (http://web.cn.edu/kwheeler/resource_rhet.html).

When students move from the focus lesson provided to an examination of Dr. King's speech and an essay that duplicates his argument, teachers must spend some time on the concept of rhetoric. A lengthy examination of this topic is not recommended, but students should understand that rhetoric was devised by the ancient Greeks and is still a part of intelligent and well-reasoned argument today. They should understand the concept of assumptions, looking for rival assumptions, and explaining how their view accounts for rival views.

Acquiring Skills in Language Usage

According to Killgallon and Killgallon (2007), there are a few simple strategies that novice writers can be taught to improve their writing. The first is to provide examples from literature that illustrate the skill the students are learning. Students must first understand the model in terms of the skill being taught. Some students may profit from copying the model, or matching the parts of the model to reassemble the original, but everyone must understand the fundamental issue in the model before being ready to move to the next step.

The next step involves unscrambling models of the skill and asking students to put the pieces together correctly. Educators will find this process especially helpful for students who need multiple strategies to improve their writing skills. Finally, the students are asked to imitate the model to demonstrate their mastery of the new skill.

Handout 1: Practicing Parallel Structure

According to *The Little, Brown Handbook* (Fowler & Aaron, 2012, p. 420), parallelism requires that all parts of the sentence that have similar form and function should have the same grammatical form.

Model #1

"The pioneers passed through the town and
into the vast, unpopulated desert"

Model # 2

"The air is dirtied by factories belching smoke and
cars spewing exhaust."

1. Students who would profit from the experience can copy the models and highlight the examples of parallel structure.

2. Students who do not need to copy the original can participate in the following matching activity:

"The industrial base was	shifting sinking
Three reasons why steel companies were losing money were	high labor costs inefficient plants increased competition" (p. 421)

3. When all students have mastered the ability to recognize parallel structures, it is time to use the following to help improve their skills:

<u>Match and underline</u> the parallel structure in each complete sentence.

Mark Twain refused	1. but a tax relief (FDR).
Huck Finn learns	2. to ignore the blindness of society or spare the reader's sensibilities
It is not a tax bill	3. not only that human beings have enormous capacity for folly, but also enormous dignity.
At the end of the novel, Huck Finn	4. both rejects society's values and affirms his own values.

4. <u>Imitating a model</u>. Students will be given the following parallel sentences and will rewrite each in their own words using parallel structure for every example.
   a. The study found that most welfare recipients wanted to work rather than to accept handouts (p. 425).
   b. Eating an animal has not always been an automatic or an everyday affair; it has tended to be done on solemn occasions and for a special treat (Margaret Visser, as cited in *The Little, Brown Handbook*, p. 424).

5. Students will write their own sentences demonstrating parallel structure and will underline each part of the sentence that is parallel.

Note: Exercises of this nature should be a part of every follow-up lesson plan so the students have multiple opportunities to practice using parallel structures in their writing.

"LETTER FROM BIRMINGHAM JAIL"

Although many students have heard of Dr. King and his work in the civil rights movement in the 1960s, it is important to provide some background information before beginning to teach this letter. A very simple timeline the students can use to read and understand the letter in its historical context will be helpful. During motivational activities, this is a good exercise for clearing up students' misunderstandings regarding this time period.

Timeline

1	2	3
Good Friday April 12, 1963 MLK arrested	April 16, 1963 Letter written on margins of a newspaper	November 1963 JFK, first Catholic president, shot

Using this timeline, teachers can ask their students working in their teams to brainstorm everything they think they know about each of these events. When the reading has been completed, teachers should return to this list and fix all of the information which needs to be corrected.

At the start of the lesson (which will probably take two or three class periods), I suggest that teachers let their students know that King was arrested for failing to obtain a parade permit from the Birmingham City Commission and for disobeying a court order which made it illegal for civil rights leaders to take part in or encourage demonstrations. It is in this context of the tyranny of segregation that Dr. King wrote one of "the classics in the literature of civil disobedience from the inside of a jail cell" (Tiefenbrun, 1992, p. 255).

Lesson Plan—Dr. Martin Luther King Jr.: "Letter from Birmingham Jail"

Transparency is essential for engaging learners in the teaching and learning process (Porton, 2013). Therefore, teachers should use the following (table 2.1) to help their students know what they are doing in class each day, why they are doing it, what strategies they will be involved in, and how they will be assessed.

Table 2.1. Lesson Plan

Lesson Title: Understanding Literary Allusions
Lesson Unit: "Letter from Birmingham Jail"

Lesson Purpose	Purpose of lesson: Examine the Essential Question for this unit/ understand references used throughout the text
Essential Question	How does a just person make decisions in an unjust world?
CCSS Standards	**RI. 9–10. 1:** Cite strong and thorough textual evidence to support analysis of what the text says explicitly as well as inferences drawn from the text. **RI. 9–10.2:** Determine a central idea of a text and analyze its development over the course of the text, including how it emerges and is shaped and refined by specific details. **RI. 9–10.4:** Determine the meaning of words and phrases as they are used in a text, including figurative, connotative, and technical meanings; analyze the cumulative impact of specific word choices on meaning and tone. **RI. 9–10.9:** Analyze seminal U.S. documents of historical and literary significance (e.g., Washington's Farewell Address, "Letter from Birmingham Jail"), including how they address related themes and concepts.
Student Outcomes	As a result of participating in today's lesson, students will use a variety of sources to determine the meaning of the important references Dr. King uses in his letter.
LDC Template	After reading Dr. King's "Letter from Birmingham Jail," write an argument that addresses the Essential Question: How does a just person make decisions in an unjust world? and support your position with evidence from your research. Be sure to acknowledge competing views. Give examples from your research to illustrate and clarify your position.
Habits of Mind Target	"Thinking flexibly . . . being able to change perspectives, generate alternatives, consider options" (Costa & Kallick, 2009, p. x).
Materials Needed	• "Letter from Birmingham Jail," Dr. Martin Luther King • Access to Google Search and Google Scholar • The Dr. Martin Luther King Jr. Public Domain Resources Site: MLKOnline>Videos>Letter from Birmingham Jail • List of terms/references/constructs to be researched
Warm up	"If one really wishes to know how justice is administered in a country, one does not question the policemen, the lawyers, the judges, or the protected members of the middle class. One goes to the unprotected—those, precisely, who need the law's protection most!—and listens to their testimony." James Baldwin On your placemat, answer your question: 1. Why is it useless to ask the protected members of society about that society's use of justice? 2. How does asking the poor and downtrodden give a more honest picture of the society's dedication to justice?

	3. What are some of the similarities and differences in the two groups' descriptions that would lead you to believe this is a just society? 4. What are some of the similarities and differences in the two groups' descriptions that would lead you to believe this is an unjust society? 5. After each team has responded to the warm-up question, ask the students how they would begin to define justice and injustice. Have the students record their classes' answers in their journals.
Motivation	1. Have the students review the timeline your have provided, and ask them to brainstorm all the information they think they know about each item. Preserve their answers. 2. Show the video from the Dr. Martin Luther King Jr. Public Domain Resources Site: MLKOnline>Videos>Letter from Birmingham Jail. 3. As a team, brainstorm as many current examples of injustices as you can. Triage the list from most to least important. As a class, agree on the five most significant forms of injustice.
Guided Practice	Our goals for this lesson are for our students to be able to begin the process of analyzing the Essential Question for this unit, and find the necessary background information in order to do a careful reading of the text. The warm up and motivation set the stage for the first step of answering the Essential Question. We will use a jigsaw approach in the next phase of the lesson to find the necessary background information. Each team member will be assigned a number. All number 1 students will work with a temporary team and find the right answers for their references. Numbers 2, 3, and 4 will do the same. After all the temporary teams have completed their work, the students will return to their home teams and share their answers with the whole group. The teacher will model one of the items, look for it in an appropriate source, check another source to be sure the explanation is correct, and remain flexible during the search so that if the answer does not fit preconceived notions, the learner will be able to seek alternative answers and accept the correct explanation. The teacher will model this experience during guided practice and discuss with the students how to remain flexible and why it is an important skill. I will model Buber's *I and Thou* since I have spent some time trying to understand Buber (with limited success!). Terms/references/concepts needed to be researched: Group One: Southern Christian Leadership Conference Early Christians and the lions Martin Luther Thalidomide Group Two: Apostle Paul—Gospel of Jesus St. Augustine—"An unjust law is no law at all." Socrates and academic freedom John Bunyan

(continued)

Table 2.1. *(Continued)*

	Group Three: Sherriff Bull Conner Paul Tillich Laws of Nazi Germany White Citizens Council Group Four: Socrates—tension in the mind Shadrach, Meshach, and Abednego and Nebuchadnezzar Hungarian Freedom Fighters in World War II James Meredith
Independent Practice	When the original teams reunite, each student will share his/her list of terms and their application to Dr. King's letter. By the end of the lesson, each student will have a complete list of the terms and their meanings to be used for the close reading of Dr. King's letter.
Academic Assessment (10 points)	Directions to students: On your own, return to the list of the five worst injustices and review the order of the list. How and why did you change the list's order? Please include all data from today's work that affected your thinking.
Habits of Mind Assessment (5 points)	In your response, include evidence of flexibility in your thinking (5 points). The team that demonstrated the most persistence gets an additional 5 points.
Closure	Dr. King said, "Injustice anywhere is a threat to justice everywhere." How does that apply to what we have studied today?
Homework (10 points)	In your journal, write a brief entry describing your personal experiences with injustice. What did you learn from those experiences?

Daily News!

The following can be posted on the board each day. Students should be expected to read it when they enter the classroom.

Personal Reflections before Implementing the Lesson

Having just written this lesson plan (table 2.1), *I thought it would be helpful if I shared some of my reflections regarding this process with you. This is much harder work than any other lesson planning I have ever done. I had to create the scaffolding the students will need to reach the CCSS goals, and include higher-order thinking skills that students can utilize in this and future readings. To account for these problems, I think senior tutors could help all the students understand the warm up and the motivation. I suggest using a video of Dr. King reading his letter for those students who need multiple sensory experiences with all texts in today's lesson.*

Today's Goals: What will we be learning today?

CCSS RI.	9.3 Analyze how the author unfolds an analysis of events. 9.9 Analyze important U.S. documents of historical significance.
H. of M.	Remaining flexible

Today's Strategies: What activities will we use to help us reach our goals?

1	Initial analysis of the Essential Question for this unit
2	Jigsaw

Materials Needed: "Letter from Birmingham Jail," Dr. Martin Luther King Jr.
List of terms to be researched

Today's Assessment: How will I know if each of you reached our goals?

Paper-pencil?	Demonstration?	One-on-one response with me?	Teamwork?
X			**X**

Assessments: Written assessment (10 points)—CCSS
Evidence of flexible thinking in assessment (5 points)—HofM
Evidence of flexible thinking in classroom discussions (5 points) —HofM
Homework (10 points)

Next, I had to consider which Habits of the Mind skill corresponds best with the day's academic goals. Struggling learners are frequently rigid thinkers. According to a study conducted by Schotte and Clum (1982), there is a relationship between negative life stress, cognitive rigidity, and/or poor problem-solving skills.

Therefore, I selected flexible thinking as the Habits of Mind skill for this reading selection. From the very beginning of their high school experiences, at-risk students need to become more resilient and flexible if they are to attempt the challenges that are integral to CCSS. In addition, if the Habits of Mind and academic goals are not aligned, the strategies and assessments can overwhelm the students and neither goal will be accomplished.

The follow-up lesson plans that need to be implemented for this lesson should include differentiation and practice on using the references in meaningful activities so that the students have substantial understanding of the most important references used in the letter.

For differentiation purposes, I am just reviewing a process that is frequently used. After a whole group instruction lesson, the day's assessment results are used to determine which students gained mastery, which students struggled, and which students displayed very little or no mastery. The warm up and some of the strategies used for the following lesson should provide extension, practice, and re-teaching to those students who need each type of response. Every daily assessment is used following the same pattern so that no student is permanently locked into remediation whether she needs it or not.

The next whole group lesson plan will be the close reading of the text using all of the effective reading strategies that will help students read for declarative understanding, inferences, nuances, and recognition of Dr. King's claims, evidence, and warrants, and King's response to our Essential Question: How does a just person make decisions in an unjust world?

When I teach this lesson, I want to be sure all assignments give students experience with rigorous texts, meaningful classroom experiences, and opportunities for creative and independent thinking. This lesson provides a unique opportunity for students to interact with a rigorous text that still has meaning today.

CREATING A REASONABLE ARGUMENT

As difficult as it can be to encourage students to read challenging texts, getting them to write a well-elaborated response can be an absolute nightmare. Students who have negative self-concepts, low self-esteem, and a compromised sense of self-efficacy are frequently unwilling to attempt challenging tasks because they "have come to see themselves often as 'dumb' rather than unskilled. . . . Dumbness, goes the reasoning, cannot be cured so adults give up on them and the kids give up on themselves" (Sagor, 1993, pp. 11–12).

In this context, teachers must first address the students' negative and dismissive attitudes about school. The literature is filled with information regarding motivational theories, but for these purposes, two major constructs—cognitive dissonance and providing choices and rewards as central to motivation—have the most utility.

According to cognitive dissonance theory as applied in education, students often assume a role, for example, class clown, class brain, class goof-off. These roles tend to be reinforced by the behavior demonstrated by the child, and the student's attitude. If all of these states remain unchanged, the child is in reduced stress. However, if any one of these changes, cognitive dissonance occurs, and the child experiences stress. Teachers want to create cognitive dissonance. The best and most effective way to accomplish that task is to help the child to change his behavior so that his attitude and role must come into alignment in order to reduce the stress (Sagor, 1993).

Therefore, by engaging students in focus lesson plans before they begin sophisticated and demanding learning tasks, teachers give them a chance to change their behavior from "I will not try" to "I will do this." When the behavior moves, the attitude and role of the "dumb" kid have to adjust to diminish the stress caused by the cognitive dissonance.

Neuroscience has viewed the issue of motivational theory from a different perspective. Van Leijenhorst, Zanolie, Van Meel, Westenberg, Rombouts, and Crone (2009) found that during adolescence brain activity increases when there is a reward offered for a given behavior. Providing students with choices may be an alternative to rewards for motivating youngsters. In my classroom, I tried to provide both since my students' self-esteem and self-efficacy were so low that neither choice nor reward alone was sufficient.

When the two theories are combined, a formula for moving students from reluctant (at best) writers to students who know how to and can write sophisticated responses to rigorous texts has been created. First, using the focus lesson, teachers can move behavior from "I won't" to "I will try." Choices and rewards are important for helping students make this essential transition. Once the students have begun to try, and the students gain confidence, teachers can help them to write on the level that the CCSS requires.

Focus Lesson

Ultimately, the students will be writing an argument in response to Dr. King's letter. However, they may not know how to make claims, find supporting evidence, and create warrants. The purpose of a focus lesson is to take the content out of the teaching/learning process, and practice the requisite skills with a topic of high interest to the students.

For this focus lesson (tables 2.2–2.4), the following issues will be provided. Each student will select the topic that has the most interest for her. The model used will provide the scaffolding for each child to be able to create a claim. "A claim is a statement that you are asking the other person to accept. This includes information you are asking them to accept as true or actions you want them to accept and enact" (http://changingminds.org/disciplines/argument/making_argument/toulmin.htm, p. 1).

Once the students have selected their topics and created their claims based on the model provided, they are ready to learn how to find evidence to support their claims. Issues such as credible and reliable sources must be addressed, the relationship between evidence and claim must be modeled, and students must be given sufficient time and access to information to find reliable sources to support their claims.

The final step is the most difficult and requires an additional class period in order to help students practice writing warrants. "A warrant links data and other grounds to a claim, legitimizing the claim by showing the grounds to be relevant. . . . It answers the question: 'Why does that data mean your claim is true?'" (http://changingminds.org/disciplines/, p. 1).

Suggested topics for the focus lesson can include, but are not limited to, the following:

1. The rights of smokers vs. the rights of non-smokers,
2. High school graduates and required military service,
3. Police officers and the use of lethal force to protect the public,
4. The effects of dropouts on their communities.

Reflections on Writing This Lesson

The task at hand was for me to break down this process into manageable chunks so that the students can understand the skill required for writing claims, practice the skill, and improve their ability to demonstrate this skill without feeling overwhelmed. I had to create a positive climate so that the students' behavior would indicate a willingness to try, provide real and interesting choices for the students, and find a meaningful reward for hard work. Many struggling learners have been taught very formulaic writing strategies that do not encourage creative or independent thinking.

Follow-up lessons should provide students with multiple opportunities for developing the skills required for finding useful and valid evidence to support the claim and creating follow-up sentences that connect the claim to the Essential Question. Finally, the students should begin categorizing the evidence into three broad examples that prove the point of the argument. I suggest using a least- to most-important organizational strategy since it allows students to make their own decisions regarding the relative importance of each of their examples and support those choices in their essays.

Table 2.2. Focus Lesson Plan: Writing Arguments

Lesson Purpose **Essential Question**	Understand how to write a credible argument using **claims**, evidence, and warrants. How does a just person make decisions in an unjust world?
CCSS Standard	Text types and purposes
LDC Template	After reading Dr. King's "Letter from Birmingham Jail," write an argument that addresses the Essential Question: How does a just person make decisions in an unjust world? and support your position with evidence from your research. Be sure to acknowledge competing views. Give examples from your research to illustrate and clarify your position.
Academic CCSS Objectives for Instruction	**W. 9–10.1**: Write arguments to support claims using valid reasoning and sufficient evidence. **1 a:** Introduce precise claims, distinguish claims from alternate or opposing claims, and create an organization that establishes clear relationships among claims . . . and evidence. **1 b:** Develop claims and counterclaims fairly, supplying evidence for each while pointing out the strengths and limitations of both in a manner that anticipates the audience's knowledge level and concerns. **SL. 9–10.2:** Integrate multiple sources of information provided in diverse media or formats, evaluating the credibility and accuracy of each source. **L. 9–10.1:** Demonstrate command of the conventions of standard English grammar and usage when writing or speaking (9th grade). Use of parallel structure.
Habits of Mind Target	Persisting. Stick to it! Persevering in a task through completion; remaining focused; looking for ways to reach your goal when stuck; not giving up (Costa & Kallick, 2009, p. x).
Materials Needed	List of choices for essays Access to computers for every student
Warm up	Our class has been given the task of providing a well-thought out argument that supports a controversial topic. With your team, read over the list of choices provided and be sure everyone understands what each one means. Write a question for any topic that is not clear to you. As a class, we will be sure that each topic is clear and every team's questions have been answered.
Motivation	All of the topics listed are involved with justice in one way or another. The team that can make the best connections between one topic and justice will be given 5 extra points for their work today.

(continued)

Table 2.2. *(Continued)*

Guided Practice	My choice for this lesson is the effect of dropouts on their communities. I will create a claim based on my position regarding this topic. My claim is as follows: High school dropouts create serious problems for themselves and their communities. • This claim asserts that high school dropouts cause real difficulties for everyone in their communities, including themselves. I took the topic listed and added my position to create my claim.
Independent Practice	Each student will choose one of the topics and create a claim based on his beliefs regarding the topic.
Guided Practice	I will model how to find credible evidence to support my claim. I will use Google, Google Scholar, and/or other search engines to find my evidence. Google Search: 1. "Crime Linked to Dropout Rates, Report Says," by SLJ Staff—*School Library Journal*, August 27, 2008. 2. Study Finds High Rate of Imprisonment among Dropouts, by Sam Dillon. Published: October 8, 2009. 3. Broad Foundation Findings: • The poverty rate for families headed by dropouts is more than twice that of families headed by high school graduates. • Nearly 44 percent of dropouts under age 24 are jobless, and the unemployment rate of high school dropouts older than 25 is more than three times that of college graduates. • Over a lifetime, dropouts earn $260,000 less than high school graduates. • The health of an 18-year-old high school dropout is similar to that of a more educated person over two decades older. • In the United States, high school dropouts commit about 75 percent of the crimes. 4. "Facing the School Dropout Dilemma," American Psychological Association. *Note:* *It took me less than five minutes using only Google to find this body of evidence. I will show my students exactly how I made each choice.* Next, I will write a few sentences that connect my claim to the Essential Question—how does a just person make decisions in an unjust world? Model: When an individual decides to drop out of school, that person has a negative impact not only on himself, but on his whole community. (claim) Although the decision to drop out of school prior to receiving a high school diploma may appear to be the right of any individual, the data clearly indicate that everyone in the dropout's community will be paying for what is essentially one person's poor decision. In a truly just world, people should take responsibility for their actions and be willing to accept all the benefits and burdens that accompany their choices. (connection between claim and justice)

	In order to introduce the concept of parallel structure, the students will use Handout 1. After this, each lesson plan should provide practice on writing using parallel structure. The first handout provides all the steps required for helping students acquire this skill. Student work should demonstrate improved student performance regarding this skill.
Independent Practice	Depending on each student's skill level, either working alone or with a senior tutor, or the educator, each student will find four to five pieces of evidence to support her/his claim. The evidence must be related to the topic chosen and to the theme of justice we are studying.
Assessment (5 points)	Write a few sentences connecting your claim to the Essential Question. You can use my model to help you. The team that made the best connections between our topics and justice will get an additional 5 points.
Habits of Mind Assessment (10 points)	Each student who demonstrated persistence in spite of the difficulty of this lesson will be given 10 points. Persistence points are earned by doing the work, not giving up, asking for help, and refraining from being off-task to avoid the work.
Closure	What is the difference between using facts to support your claims and using only opinions?
Homework (5 points)	Look for any more evidence you can find to support your claim or write a few more sentences to connect another claim to your evidence.

Handout 2—Using the MLA Citation System

Verbatim Quotes

- If you are using the exact words of the writer and putting them in your own paper, you must follow this system:
  - Dr. King said, "We can never forget that everything Hitler did in Germany was legal" (3).
    - Quote—"We can never forget that everything Hitler did in Germany was legal."
    - We use quotation marks to indicate that this is a direct quote.
    - King—the author of the quote.
    - 3—the page number where the quote can be found.
  - According to an article in the *Wall Street Journal*, November 13, 1962, Dr. King said: "It may be true that the law cannot make a man love me, but it can keep him from lynching me, and I think that's pretty important" (http://about.com).
    - Quote indicated by quotation marks.
    - No page is available, but web address is provided.

Paraphrased Quotes

- If you are putting the quote into your own words, you must give credit to the original author.
    - Dr. King reminded us in his "Letter from Birmingham Jail" that being legal and being just are not the same thing. He used the example of the legal treatment of Jews in Nazi Germany as the most odious example of what is legal under the law and what is just (3).
        - We are no longer using King's own words, but he made the original claim and must be given credit.
        - Dr. King (3) provides the readers with the source of the information, but since there are no quotation marks, the reader knows you have put this idea in your own words.

Reflections before Teaching This Lesson

I had to create a reasonable claim that my students could understand and connect to justice. Since I will provide background knowledge to the class I will teach this to, I will explain my connection to the Holocaust and why I completely agree with Wiesel's claim. Next, I want to be sure that I have provided enough modeling and practicing experiences for all the students. If I teach this lesson, I will be especially interested in this aspect of the lesson plan.

The follow-up lessons should allow students to practice the following skills:

1. *Paraphrasing quotes to put their claims in their own words.*
2. *Writing citations for verbatim and paraphrased quotes.*
3. *Grouping their evidence into three categories, arranging them from least to most important, and supporting those decisions.*

Teaching Warrants

At this point, students should have a thorough understanding of claims and evidence. They should be able to select reliable sources and begin to draw connections between their claims and their evidence. However, warrants require another level of sophistication; I suggest teaching how to write warrants in a discrete lesson. Let us review the definition of a warrant: "A warrant links data and other grounds to a claim, legitimizing the claim by showing the grounds to be relevant" (http://changingminds.org/disciplines/argument/making_argument/toulmin.htm, p. 1).

Table 2.3. Lesson Plan: Creating a Coherent Argument

Lesson Purpose **Essential Question**	Understand how to write a credible argument using **claims**, **evidence**, and warrants. How does a just person make decisions in an unjust world?
CCSS Standard	Text types and purposes
LDC Template	After reading Dr. King's "Letter from Birmingham Jail," write an argument that addresses the Essential Question: How does a just person make decisions in an unjust world? and support your position with evidence from your research. Be sure to acknowledge competing views. Give examples from your research to illustrate and clarify your position.
Academic CCSS Objectives for Instruction	**W. 9–10.1:** Write arguments to support claims using valid reasoning and sufficient evidence. **1 a:** Introduce precise claims, distinguish claims from alternate or opposing claims, and create an organization that establishes clear relationships among claims . . . and evidence. **1 b:** Develop claims and counterclaims fairly, supplying evidence for each while pointing out the strengths and limitations of both in a manner that anticipates the audience's knowledge level and concerns. **W. 9–10.8:** Gather relevant information from multiple authoritative print and digital sources, using advanced searches effectively, assess the usefulness of each source in answering the research question; integrate information into the text selectively to maintain the flow of ideas, avoiding plagiarism, and following a standard format for citation. **SL. 9–10.2:** Integrate multiple sources of information provided in diverse media or formats, evaluating the credibility and accuracy of each source.
Habits of Mind Target	Persisting. Stick to it! Persevering in a task through completion; remaining focused; looking for ways to reach your goal when stuck; not giving up (Costa & Kallick, 2009, p. x).
Materials Needed	Copy of "Letter from Birmingham Jail" Smart Board Access to computers
Warm up	With your team, find Dr. King's essential claim in the letter. Discuss the reasons for your choice.
Motivation	What are some of the assumptions that Dr. King makes in his claim? What are the opposing assumptions? Can you convince people to change their minds if they believe in their side just as strongly as you believe in yours? Explain.
Guided Practice Making a Claim	I will model how to create a claim regarding justice. In a speech given in 2006, Elie Wiesel said: "To remain silent and indifferent is the greatest sin of all" (http://theloquitur.com/). I really agree. I have to take Wiesel's quote and make my own claim based on its truth to me.

(continued)

Table 2.3. *Continued*

	When terrible things are done to innocent people, those who stand by and do nothing are demonstrating the greatest sin of all: indifference (Wiesel 2008). I simply reorganized Wiesel's thought and put it in my own words. Next, I have to demonstrate how to decide if my data is useful. I like Hillocks (2011) simple strategy: 1. Examine data 2. Ask questions based on data 3. Reexamine data 4. Try to answer the questions 5. Data that supports our answer = Evidence (p. xxii).
Independent Practice	• Using an aide, special educator, senior tutor, and/or general educator, the students will research quotes about justice and select one they agree with. • Next, they will find a quote that expresses their ideas, and paraphrase it to make their initial claim. • Claims must meet the criteria we studied in the focus lesson. • Sentences following claims must link the claim to the Essential Question.
Guided Practice Finding Evidence	Using Google, Google Scholar, and/or other search engines, I will look up supporting evidence for my claim. I start by looking up indifference and evil. Google Search: 1. "The UN Security Council, Indifference, and Genocide in Rwanda," Michael N. Barnett. Article first published online: January 7, 2008, DOI: 10.1525/can.1997.12.4.551, volume 12, issue 4, pp. 551–78, November 1997. 2. *Stories, Ethics and Indifference*, B. Hucker, 1998, Tayler & Francis. 3. "The Pole of Power and the Pole of Indifference," Arnold Wolfers, Yale University. 4. "Journeying through the Valley of Evil," D.O. Lindner, *North Carolina Law Review*, April 1992. 5. "Letter from Birmingham Jail" (King, 3). *Note:* I will do a think aloud as I view each entry. I will discuss why I selected some articles rather than others. I will explain why I cannot use Elie Wiesel to prove my point since we cannot use our source to provide our evidence. Next, I will provide a simple MLA handout to help students use appropriate citations for their sources (see Handout 1).
Independent Practice	Using all the support each student needs, every student will look through the search engines to begin finding evidence to support his claims. Students will practice writing citations for each source. Each team will put its best evidence and citation on the Smart Board for all of us to see.

Assessment (10 points)	By yourself, use a search engine to find one good piece of evidence to support the claim that Dr. King believed that Kennedy's assassination was a result of the hatred that existed in America at that time. Create a citation for that source.
Habits of Mind Assessment (10 points) **Team 5**	Each student (10) and each team (5) that demonstrated persistence in spite of the difficulty of this lesson will be given up to 15 points. Persistence points are earned by doing the work, not giving up, asking for help, and refraining from being off-task to avoid the work. The team that does the best job of helping each other during the search and citation process will earn an additional 5 points.
Closure	What was the most challenging part of today's lesson?
Homework (5 points)	Either continue to look for more sources or work on your claim to make it sound even stronger.

Let us use the claim made that high school dropouts create problems for themselves and their broader community. If one only listed the data found during the Google search, the claim would only be restated. However, if one added warrants, one could make the argument clearer by showing how the decision to drop out of school can be correlated with disastrous outcomes.

Claim: High school dropouts create serious problems for themselves and their communities.

Evidence: The poverty rate for families headed by dropouts is more than twice that of families headed by high school graduates.
Over a lifetime, dropouts earn $260,000 less than high school graduates.

Warrant: A person's decision to drop out of school does not only affect that person, it becomes a problem and a burden for his community as well.
Because of limitations in job opportunities and advancement in employment, and their likelihood of extended unemployment, dropouts are not self-sufficient and usually the broader community is burdened with the costs of supporting them and their families.

It is up to teachers when to teach this lesson (table 2.4) to their students. Because it requires higher-order thinking skills as well as a certain degree of writing mastery, I suggest it is taught after the students are comfortable writing claims and finding good evidence. The follow-up lessons should include writing warrants and acknowledging

Table 2.4. Lesson Plan: Warrants

Lesson Purpose	Understand how to write a credible argument using claims, evidence, and **warrants**.
Essential Question	How does a just person make decisions in an unjust world?
CCSS Standard	Text types and purposes
LDC Template	After reading Dr. King's "Letter from Birmingham Jail," write an argument that addresses the Essential Question: How does a just person make decisions in an unjust world? and support your position with evidence from your research. Be sure to acknowledge competing views. Give examples from your research to illustrate and clarify your position.
Academic CCSS Objectives for Instruction	**W. 9–10.1:** Write arguments to support claims using valid reasoning and sufficient evidence. **1 a:** Introduce precise claims, distinguish claims from alternate or opposing claims, and create an organization that establishes clear relationships among claims, reasons, and evidence. **1 b:** Develop claims and counterclaims fairly, supplying evidence for each while pointing out the strengths and limitations of both in a manner that anticipates the audience's knowledge level and concerns. **SL. 9–10.2:** Integrate multiple sources of information provided in diverse media or formats, evaluating the credibility and accuracy of each source. **SL. 9–10.4:** Present information, findings, and supporting evidence clearly, concisely, and logically such that listeners can follow the line of reasoning and the organization, development, substance, and style are appropriate to purpose, audience, and task.
Habits of Mind Target	Persisting. Stick to it! Persevering in a task through completion; remaining focused; looking for ways to reach your goal when stuck; not giving up (Costa & Kallick, 2009, p. x).
Materials Needed	Access to computers
Warm up	With your teams, answer the following questions: 1. What is the difference between a claim and evidence? 2. How do you know when your evidence is useful? 3. Why is it important to use reliable sources for your evidence? 4. How can you respond to good points from the opposite view?
Motivation	Respond to this statement and tell me what you think of it: Native Americans walk in single file. I saw a Native American walking down my street and that's what he did. The team that finds the most flaws in this argument wins a prize.
Guided Practice	I will use my model describing dropouts to demonstrate how to connect claims and evidence together with warrants.
Independent Practice	Each person on the team will create a warrant for one piece of evidence and claim. The team will select the best one and share it with the class.

Guided Practice Creating Warrants	I will choose the best example from the teams' work and ask the student to explain how he created the warrant.
Independent Practice	The students will return to their own writing and try another example.
Assessment (10 points)	Students will create one more warrant for a different claim and evidence.
Habits of Mind Assessment (10 points)	Each student who demonstrated persistence in spite of the difficulty of this lesson will be given 10 points. Persistence points are earned by doing the work, not giving up, asking for help, and refraining from being off-task to avoid the work.
Closure	How do warrants help us to write stronger arguments?
Homework (5 points)	Write one more warrant connecting your claim to your evidence.

the valid position of the opposing views, but providing counterevidence to support the student's claims.

PUTTING IT ALL TOGETHER

When teachers believe that their students have had sufficient practice at writing claims, evidence, and warrants, they are ready to begin the summative assessment for this unit. Writing an argument that fulfills the CCSS requirements is the students' culminating activity (see table 2.5). Teachers will continue to provide scaffolding during the writing process, but this time the final draft is to be used to assess each student's mastery of all the skills they have been learning.

Rubric for Summative Assessment

For these purposes, the English/Language Arts, Grade 9, Performance Assessment Rubric (table 2.6) created by the Los Angeles Unified School District (2001) has been chosen. It takes into account the CCSS and provides a clear picture of the target so that every student knows what is required for success.

Of course, converting points to grades is very easy. Four = A; three = B or C; two = D; one = F. Students should be provided time to work on their rough drafts in class, and peer editing using the rubric should be

Table 2.5. Lesson Plan: Writing an Argument regarding Justice

Lesson Purpose	Begin work on the summary assessment.
Essential Question	How does a just person make decisions in an unjust world?
CCSS Standards	Informational Text—Key Ideas and Details and Integration of Knowledge and Ideas Writing—Text Types and Purposes Speaking and Listening—Comprehension and Collaboration Language—Parallel Structure
LDC Template	After reading Dr. King's "Letter from Birmingham Jail," write an argument that addresses the Essential Question: How does a just person make decisions in an unjust world? and support your position with evidence from your research. Be sure to acknowledge competing views. Give examples from your research to illustrate and clarify your position.
Academic CCSS Objectives for Instruction	**RI. 9–10.1:** Cite strong and thorough textual evidence to support analysis of what the text says explicitly as well as inferences drawn from the text. **RI. 9–10.3:** Analyze how the author unfolds an analysis or series of ideas or events, including the order in which the points are made, how they are introduced and developed, and the connections that are drawn between them. **RI. 9–10.6:** Determine an author's point of view or purpose in a text and analyze how an author uses rhetoric to advance that point of view or purpose. **RI. 9–10.9:** Analyze seminal U.S. documents of historical and literary significance (e.g., Washington's Farewell Address, "Letter from Birmingham Jail"), including how they address related themes and concepts. **W. 9–10.4:** Produce clear and coherent writing in which the development, organization, and style are appropriate to task, purpose, and audience. **W. 9–10.8:** Gather relevant information from multiple authoritative print and digital sources; using advanced searches effectively, assess the usefulness of each source in answering the research question; integrate information into the text selectively to maintain the flow of ideas, avoiding plagiarism and following a standard format for citation. **SL. 9–10.2:** Integrate multiple sources of information provided in diverse media or formats, evaluating the credibility and accuracy of each source. **SL. 9–10.4:** Present information, findings, and supporting evidence clearly, concisely, and logically such that listeners can follow the line of reasoning and the organization, development, substance, and style are appropriate to purpose, audience, and task. **L. 9–10.1:** Demonstrate command of the conventions of standard English grammar and usage when writing or speaking (9th grade). Use parallel structure.

Habits of Mind Target	Thinking flexibly and persisting
Materials Needed	Copies of "Letter from Birmingham Jail" Notes from claims, evidence, and warrants All returned and evaluated student work Practice materials for writing using parallel structure Rubric for final draft
Warm up	With your team, review the original list of injustices our class created the first day of this unit (teacher will provide if necessary). 1. Did we miss any examples of injustice that should have been included? 2. Have we developed a more mature understanding of injustice since this unit began? Explain in detail. 3. How does using claims, evidence, and warrants strengthen your problem-solving skills? 4. What do you think is the greatest injustice of all? Explain!
Motivation	During this unit, we have wrestled with serious and significant topics. Why did we spend so much time on justice and making decisions regarding justice? What have you learned that you will use?
Guided Practice	Our class has been studying the Essential Question: How does a just person make decisions in an unjust world? You are going to create a four-paragraph argument that states your position on one issue regarding justice in today's world. Your audience is Dr. King's son, who is still alive. Your purpose is to make a claim regarding justice, provide evidence to support your claim, and tie the evidence to your claim with sufficient warrants to make your argument convincing. In addition, you will acknowledge competing views and provide counterevidence that supports your claim. My model will be as follows: Dr. King once said, "A right delayed is a right denied" (http://www.brainyquote.com/quotes/authors/m/martin_luther_king_jr.html#). Ever since the establishment of slavery, the rights of Negroes have been summarily denied in the United States. For example, Dr. King was jailed for insisting on holding a protest meeting to ask for equal civil rights in Birmingham, Alabama, as recently as 1963, but the City Council of Birmingham refused to allow the protest and denied Dr. King and his followers the right to assemble as guaranteed in the Constitution (First Amendment, United States Constitution). Every American is supposed to be protected by the Constitution, but by delaying the rights of blacks to peacefully assemble through the use of unconstitutional city by-laws, the rights of all people of color were denied. In this essay, I will provide three other examples of delayed rights that have resulted in denying equal justice under the law to minority groups in the United States and throughout the world.

(continued)

Table 2.5. *(Continued)*

	The Arab Spring of 2011 has provided ample evidence of the disastrous results of justice denied, the treatment of Hispanic minorities under the law in the American Southwest will surely be viewed by future generations as a low point in modern American democracy, and finally, the worst example is the ongoing struggle of people of color to receive equal rights in the United States today, as illustrated by the death of an unarmed teenager whose murderer was not arrested or kept in jail after the murder despite the fact that the man immediately confessed to the crime. Language Skills—Using parallel structures (see Handout 1).
Independent Practice	Look for a quote on any search engine to use as the opening statement related to your topic. Elaborate on the connection between your claim and justice. Describe the three examples that prove your claim and put them in rank order from least to most important.
Assessment (10 points)	By yourself, write the first sentence of your second paragraph, which will be your first claim. Make sure there are no errors in the parallel structure of your sentences.
Habits of Mind Assessment (10 points)	Being flexible by looking for a good quote and persisting until you find one that fits your topic. Use informal assessment procedures.
Closure	What is the most challenging part of this process? Why?

a part of the writing process. However, the final draft is the summative assessment and is not to be returned to the students for revision.

POINTS TO PONDER

This chapter is not nor could it be a complete guide to writing every lesson plan needed for developing the skills that have been targeted. It is hoped that the models provided can help to guide busy educators through the difficult process of revamping their lesson plans to reflect the rigorous demands made by the Common Core State Standards. Even after forty-six years of experience, this has been a daunting task. Teachers can use these lesson plans as models, references, and starting points in the pursuit of helping students master the CCSS.

Table 2.6. Performance Assessment Rubric

Score 4 Advanced	• The response demonstrates well-developed comprehension of the connection between claims, evidence, and warrants. • The reasoning provided is logical and ideas are well supported by evidence. • The connection between claims and evidence through the use of warrants is clear and logical. • The connection between the claim and justice is well defined and described. • The writing indicates that the student has gathered relevant information from multiple authoritative print and digital sources, using advanced searches effectively, and assessed the usefulness of each source in answering the research question. • The writing demonstrates that the information is well integrated into the text selectively to maintain the flow of ideas, avoiding plagiarism and following a standard format for citations. • All sentences are parallel in structure.
Score 3 Proficient	• The response demonstrates a clear understanding of the connection between claims, evidence, and warrants, but there is not the level of sophistication in thinking and writing that is found in the advanced response. • The reasoning provided is usually logical and most ideas are supported by evidence. • Warrants are used to connect claims and evidence. • There is a connection between the claim and justice. • The writing indicates that the student has gathered some relevant information from multiple authoritative print and digital sources, using advanced searches, and assessed the usefulness of most sources in answering the research question. • The writing demonstrates that the information is usually integrated into the text and the flow of ideas is apparent. The student has avoided plagiarism, and the writing follows a standard format for citations. • Most sentences are parallel in structure.
Score 2 Partially Proficient	• The response demonstrates some understanding of the connection between claims, evidence, and warrants, but there is evidence that the writer does not have real mastery of this concept. • The reasoning provided is logical at times and some ideas are supported by evidence. • Warrants are not used consistently to connect claims and evidence. • There is a weak connection between the claim and justice. • The writing indicates that the student has gathered a little relevant information from multiple print and digital sources, using advanced searches, and assessed the usefulness of some, but not all, sources in answering the research question. • The writing demonstrates that the information is not well integrated into the text and the flow of ideas is not always apparent. The student has avoided plagiarism, and the writing follows a standard format for citations. • Some sentences are parallel in structure.

Score 1 Not Proficient	• The response demonstrates little or no understanding of the connection between claims, evidence, and warrants. • The reasoning provided is illogical at times and few ideas are supported by evidence. • Warrants are not used to connect claims and evidence. • There is no connection between the claim and justice. • The writing indicates that the student has gathered very little if any relevant information from multiple print and digital sources. Instead of data, opinions are offered to support the claim. • The writing demonstrates that the information is not integrated into the text and the flow of ideas is not apparent. The student has not avoided plagiarism, and/or the writing does not include the standard format for citations. • There is no evidence that parallel structure has been mastered.

REFLECTIONS

Revamping trusted lesson plans and retooling valued teaching techniques can be a daunting and stressful task. By yourself or with a partner, respond to the following:

1. What is the role of the Essential Question in the planning process?
2. How can lessons on justice affect at-risk students' thinking? Behaving?
3. How will you use claims, evidence, and warrants in your content?
4. What new strategies will you use to help your struggling learners?
5. What are the biggest challenges to you as you undertake the implementation of CCSS?

REFERENCES

Caufmann, J. C., & Steinberg (2009). (Im)maturity of judgment in adolescence: Why adolescents may be less culpable than adults. http://onlinelibrary.wiley.com/doi/10.1002/bsl.416/abstract.

Costa, A. L., & Kallick, B. (2009). Habits of mind across the curriculum. Alexandria, VA: ASCD.

Fehr, E., Rützler, D., & Sutter, M. (2011). The development of egalitarianism, altruism, spite and parochialism in childhood and adolescence. Bonn, Germany: I2A.

Fowler, H. R., & Aaron, J. E. (2012). *The little, brown handbook*. Boston: Pearson.

Immordino-Yang, M. H. & Damasio, A. (2007). We feel, therefore we learn: The relevance of affective and social neuroscience to education, mind, brain, and education, 1: 3–10.

home.comcast.net/~cphenlymbk2006/IBMA/claim-evidence-warrant[1].pdf

http://changingmindsorg/disciplines/argumentmaking.

http://brainyquotes.

http://grammar.about.com/od/rhetorictoolkit/Tool_Kit_for_Rhetorical_Analysis.htm.fma.

Hu, H., Real, E., Takamiya, K., Kang, M. G., Ledoux, J. Huganir, R. L., & Manilow, R. (2007). Emotion enhances learning via norepinephrine regulation of AMPA-Receptor trafficking. www.sciencedirect.com/science/article/pii/S0092867407012056.

Immordino-Yang, M. H. & Damasio, A. (2007). We feel, therefore we learn: The relevance of affective and social neuroscience to education, mind, brain, and education, 1: 3–10.

Killgallon, D., & Killgallon, J. (2007). *Grammar for high school: A sentence-composing approach*. Portsmouth, NH: Heinemann.

King, M. L., Jr. (1963). Letter from Birmingham Jail. April 16, 1963.

Porton, H. D. (2013). *Helping struggling learners succeed in school*. Boston: Pearson.

Sagor, R. (1993). *At-risk students: Reaching and teaching them.* Boston: Pearson.

Schotte, D. E., & Clum, G. A. (1982). Suicide ideation in a college population: A test of a model. *Journal of Consulting and Clinical Psychology, 50*(5), 690–696.

Stiehm, J. Oval Office rug gets history wrong. *Washington Post*, September 4, 2010. www.washingtonpost.com/wp-dyn/content/article/2010/09/03/AR2010090305100.html.

Sturm, D. (1984). Crisis in the American Republic: The legal and political significance of Martin Luther King's letter from a Birmingham Jail. *J. L. & Religion 309.*

Tiefenburn, S. (1992). Semiotics and Martin Luther King's "Letter from Birmingham Jail." *Cardozo Studies in Law and Literature*, 255–287.

Van Leijenhorst, Zanolie, Van Meel, C. S., Westenberg, P. M., Rombouts, S. A. R. B., and Crone, E. A. (2010). "What motivates the adolescent." Brain regions explaining neural sensitivity across adolescence. *Certeb Cortex*, 20(1), 61–69. D0I: 10.1093/cercor/bhp078. First published online: April 30, 2009.

3

HOW DO WE LEARN HOW WE ARE AND WHO WE ARE?

Jem, there's just one kind of folks. Folks.

—Harper Lee

According to Erikson, adolescence is characterized by each person's profound need to create a personal identity. During this developmental phase, most adolescents have started to develop the cognitive, emotional, and psychological awareness necessary to examine and ultimately determine the answers to the identity questions "Where did I come from?" "Who am I?" and "What do I want to become?" (as cited in Muuss, 1996, p. 51).

Essential components of forming an identity include, but are not limited to, the role of race, class, and gender in understanding that identity is shaped by each person's experience with the broader social context. In the sociological and psychological literature, "identity is commonly understood as one's personally held beliefs about the self in relation to social groups (e.g., race, ethnicity, religion, sexual orientation) and the ways one expresses that relationship" (Torres, Jones, & Renn, 2009, p. 577).

The Essential Question for this unit, which includes reading and responding to *To Kill a Mockingbird* (Lee, 1960), typically revolves around definitions of courage and honor. However, in order to help students read this amazing novel on a more sophisticated and nuanced level, the subtext of identity formation could be explored.

During the entire novel, Scout is being taught by the broader community's power structures how to behave based on her race, social class, and gender. Therefore, before and while reading the novel, teachers should use the typical approach of exploring the three dominant themes of the novel: (1) Why is it a sin to kill a mockingbird? (2) What is the real definition of courage? Honor? (3) How do we really learn to understand another person? However, the close reading of the novel should also include an explication of its less-explored, but very important subtext.

WHY STUDY IDENTITY FORMATION?

According to Flum and Kaplan, "Although there is no shortage of research interest in identity in general, and in the related conceptual space, an explicit focus on the interface of identity and education is still rare (Kaplan & Flum, 2009; Schachter & Rich, 2011)" (as cited in Flum & Kaplan, 2012, p. 241). Nevertheless, despite its paucity in teaching practices, Sinai, Kaplan, and Flum (2012) found that "Individuals who engage in identity exploration are commonly found to be open to diversity of experiences, demonstrate cognitive complexity and flexibility . . . have higher moral reasoning, and exercise self-awareness and autonomy in pursuing important life decisions" (p. 196).

None of these goals can be accomplished without the presence of a caring and supportive teacher. Teachers must create a safe classroom environment where students feel sufficiently comfortable to express themselves freely, know they will be protected and respected, and explore what matters to them. Also, teachers must be prepared to accept the uncertainty that this work requires while maintaining the healthy boundaries students need (Flum & Kaplan, 2012). This is the heart of CCSS. Students must be protected and exposed to learning experiences that extend and refine their thinking about themselves and others.

IN THIS CHAPTER

In this chapter, strategies for developing a more sophisticated understanding of the subtext of *To Kill a Mockingbird* as well as some interesting strategies for exploring the three dominant themes of the novel will be explored. A lesson plan that I used with my students for understanding others by learning how to analyze perspectives will be provided.

The plan and my reflections are included. Next, the subtext of the novel that concentrates on how Scout's identity was formed by the broader social context of her world will be discussed. For example, Calpurnia, Reverend Sykes, and Tom Robinson, as well as most of the white community of Maycomb, are exemplars for understanding how race shapes identity. The contrasts among the Finch family, the Cunninghams, and the Ewells speak to the importance of class in identity formation, and Aunt Alexander and Calpurnia's attempts to shape Scout's behavior and attitudes based on gender are explicit and ongoing.

The second half of the chapter deals with the summative writing assignment for this unit. For this assignment, students will be asked to align the three themes of the novel with the subtext to demonstrate their understanding of the novel. When they recognize that killing a mockingbird, for example, is a symbol of attacking vulnerable members of society, hopefully they are on their way to developing a personal sense of identity based on authentic demonstrations of courage, honor, and integrity.

Identity Formation

It is our interactions with others, the norms we learn that are expected by our community, and/or the expectations that result from our culture that have an intense influence on how we construct our identity (Jones, 1997; McEwen, 2003; Torres, 2003; Torres, Jones, & Renn, 2009; Weber, 1998). As Scout navigates the deceptively calm community in which she and her family live, she learns valuable life lessons about who she is, what she believes to be true about herself, and how she forms her new sense of self; therefore, Lee is able to explore Scout's beginning stages of identity formation by creating a completely seamless and convincing illustration of this process.

Erikson (1959) wrote adolescents "are sometimes morbidly, often curiously, preoccupied with what they appear to be in the eyes of others as compared with what they feel they are and with the question of how to connect to earlier cultivated roles and skills with the ideal prototype of the day" (p. 89). It is fair to say that students are very egocentric and this attempt to develop their understanding of self and others should resonate with them very well. This analysis of the novel is a good match for students' developmental trajectory and requires the higher-order thinking skills called for by CCSS.

TO KILL A MOCKINGBIRD

In this classic American novel, readers are introduced to the world of the Deep South around the time of World War II. The first person, uninvolved narrator leads readers through the story with a wonderful mixture of innocence and insight. Lee gives her readers a more sophisticated understanding of the plot by allowing Scout to eavesdrop on her father's conversations with several significant adults in the novel, especially his brother Jack. Historically, the novel's three dominant themes have served as the basis for analyzing the text.

Struggling learners normally do not struggle with the declarative knowledge presented in the novel. They need some scaffolding in terms of historical context so that they understand that the United States in the 1930s during the Depression and on the eve of World War II was considerably different from what it is in the twenty-first century. Nevertheless, the novel is considered a classic since so much of it has remained true despite the differences in time, place, and demographics.

Common Core State Standards and *To Kill a Mockingbird*

For these purposes, attention will be focused on the following CCSS standards:

RL. 9–10.1: Cite strong and thorough textual evidence to support analysis of what the text says explicitly as well as inferences drawn from the text.

RL. 9–10.2: Determine a theme or central idea of a text and analyze in detail its development over the course of the text, including how it emerges and is shaped and refined by specific details.

RL. 9–10.3: Analyze how complex characters develop over the course of a text, interact with other characters, and advance the plot or develop the theme.

SL. 9–10.1: Initiate and participate effectively in a range of collaborative discussions with diverse partners, building on others' ideas and expressing their own clearly and persuasively.

SL. 9–10.1d: Respond thoughtfully to diverse perspectives, summarize points of agreement and disagreement, and, when warranted, qualify or justify their own views and understandings and make new connections in light of the evidence and reasoning presented.

Reading the Novel to Explore Its Three Themes

When I taught the novel to my classes, I normally began with some background information regarding the time and place described in the novel. I highly recommend using "selected photographs by Dorothea Lange, taken for the Farm Security Administration during the Great Depression (Library of Congress) and America from the Great Depression to World War II: Photographs from the FSA-OWI, 1935–1945 (Library of Congress)" (Common Core, Inc., 2012, p. 15). Teachers can use http://about.com to find specific pictures of southern schools and families. I think any class would enjoy listening to music from the Great Depression. If teachers go to www.rhapsody.com they can share some music from that era with their classes. Students really need to appreciate the power of the novel's historical context on the lives of the characters.

Analyzing Perspectives

Perhaps my favorite lesson during the novel was the one I taught on analyzing perspectives. After my students had read the novel, they participated in the following lesson (table 3.1). The only changes I have made here involve inserting the CCSS standards, which were not in use at the time.

When each student came in the room, I handed him or her a folded piece of paper. When all the students read the warm up, they unfolded their papers and began answering their warm-up questions. The majority

Table 3.1. Lesson Plan

Lesson Title: Analyzing Perspectives
Lesson Unit: *To Kill a Mockingbird (TKAM)*

Lesson Purpose **Essential Question**	Analysis of the perspective of the characters in *TKAM*. How do we learn how we are and who we are?
CCSS Standards **Academic CCSS Objectives for Instruction**	**RL. 9–10.1:** Cite strong and thorough textual evidence to support analysis of what the text says explicitly as well as inferences drawn from the text. **RL. 9–10.2:** Determine a theme or central idea of a text and analyze in detail its development over the course of the text, including how it emerges and is shaped and refined by specific details. **RL. 9–10.3:** Analyze how complex characters develop over the course of a text, interact with other characters, and advance the plot or develop the theme. **SL. 9–10.1:** Initiate and participate effectively in a range of collaborative discussions with diverse partners, building on others' ideas and expressing their own clearly and persuasively. **SL. 9–10.1d:** Respond thoughtfully to diverse perspectives, summarize points of agreement and disagreement, and, when warranted, qualify or justify their own views and understandings and make new connections in light of the evidence and reasoning presented.
Habits of Mind Target	"Listening with understanding and empathy: making an effort to perceive another's point of view and emotions" (Costa & Kallick, 2009, p. x).
Student Outcomes	As a result of participating in today's lesson, students will be able to analyze the perspectives of characters in *TKAM*.
Warm up	When each student walks in the room, he or she will be given a name of one of the major characters in the novel. As that character, they will each answer the warm-up questions: 1. What really happened to Mayella? 2. What kind of man is Tom Robinson? 3. What kind of man is Atticus? 4. Who is Boo? What is he like? Each team must pick the most interesting member to answer the drill question in character. Team member number 3 has to explain why the person was chosen!
Guided Practice Time	Mrs. Porton will select a folded paper and will answer the drill questions in character. Each team has to decide the following: 1. Who is Mrs. Porton? How do you know? 2. Did Mrs. P. answer the questions accurately in character? How do you know? 3. Does Mrs. P. represent this character's attitude toward the other characters in the story accurately? How do you know?

	Next, Mrs. P. will answer a few of the interview questions in character with a pre-selected partner. Using the guided practice as our model, we will create a rubric for accuracy. The rubric will emphasize use of the text, each student's ability to answer questions from the character's perspective, and each student's willingness to forgo his/her own perceptions in favor of those of the character he or she is representing.
Independent Practice Time	Working with a teammate, each student will be interviewed in character. The partners will switch on a signal from Mrs. P. When both partners have answered all the questions, each team will select the person who did the best job using the rubric the class has just created. The entire class will watch and use the rubric to grade the four students who have been chosen to perform.
Habit of Mind	Students will be assessed on their ability to see the situations from perspectives other than their own and their use of the text to support their answers.
Closure Time	Answer in character: Who is the worst person in the novel?
Homework	Write five questions in character!

of the students were African-American, and it was inevitable that one or two of the students would have to answer as either Mayella or Bob Ewell.

Interview Questions

Directions: You will select one person on your team to be your partner. You must answer your interview questions in character, just as Mrs. Porton did. Remember everybody in Maycomb knows everyone! You will be given a few minutes to create three questions for your partner before you are told to begin. Mrs. Porton will stop by each pair to observe and evaluate each team for accuracy. Being able to listen with empathy and making an effort to see another person's point of view are part of your classroom points for today.

1. Who is Dill and why is he in Maycomb?
2. Why aren't women allowed to serve on the jury?
3. What qualities of being a lady does Scout lack?
4. Evaluate each person's job performance: Judge Taylor, Sheriff Tate, Atticus.

5. Define courage.
6. When Jem and Scout visited Old Sarum, how were they treated?
7. Whatever happened to Boo Radley? Mayella Ewell?
8. Create your own question.
9. Create your own question.
10. Create your own question.

On a Personal Note

The interview questions above had been created for the students' independent practice on situations that had taken place during the novel or that could have taken place. I drew Scout's name. The class knew who I was almost immediately. First, I answered the drill questions in character. Next, I used the interview questions with a student I had pre-selected. Again answering in character, I tried to build a framework for the rubric which we were going to create.

Following my model, in order to answer in character, students had to reason in character. By the end of independent practice, I had listened to every pair of students, and I was convinced that every student had developed the ability to suspend his or her own perspective, if only briefly, in order to see a situation from another person's point of view.

The results of the assessment question verified my anecdotal data. All of the Ewells believed that Mayella was innocent of perjury; the judge felt she should stand trial, but would be acquitted; the Robinson family felt the same, and so on. No matter what the student's race, class, and gender, when the student answered the question, the answer in character was accurate.

As we created the rubric, which was to be the scoring guide we would use to evaluate the students' answers, it was clear to me that the students understood the importance of using the text to support their answers, avoiding their own feelings when answering in character and checking for accuracy in terms of how the character would have answered the question.

One of the factors that made this lesson so memorable was the young man who had to take the role of Mayella Ewell. I could not have chosen a better set-up.

My student Earl was the most resistant of all the males in the class at trying to see anything from a female's point of view. He said he didn't have any white friends, and he only befriended me because I was his favorite teacher. Naturally, his team chose him to answer the drill question in character!

I don't remember who the number 3 person was on his team, but after Earl answered "What kind of man is Atticus?" in a falsetto voice and said that her daddy told her that Atticus is a bad man who hangs out with no-goods like other lawyers, judges, and other people who can read, the class was on the floor with laughter! He really helped me to set the stage for what was to follow! The other team's choices were just as willing to answer in character and start thinking from a different person's perspective (Porton, 2013).

When the students reflected in their end-of-the-year journal about their favorite unit and lesson, most of the class listed this lesson as their favorite. They saw the value of understanding another person's perspective in order to improve their relationships with important people in their own lives. They respected Atticus, and they learned for themselves that Atticus was right: "You never really understand a person until you consider things from his point of view—until you climb into his skin and walk around in it" (Lee, 1960, p. 30).

IDENTITY FORMATION: RACE

I would like to begin this discussion with a few stories to help illustrate my points. When my son David was a very little boy, he demonstrated an impressive imagination, intelligence, and insight. He was also a perfect model of how children learn about race to form their identity. When David was about four years old, we lived in a very diverse community in Edgewood, Maryland. Our apartment complex included a pool, and my children and I spent many lovely days there.

One day a young African-American girl came up to David and said, "You are white, and I am black." I was interested in hearing David's reply since we did not categorize people by race. David said, "I am not white." After a while, the little girl got tired of trying to convince my son that he was really white, so she brought her older sister to tell David the truth! The older child looked at David and said flatly, "Kid, you're white." The next day, I decided to check to see if this new understanding had had any effect on David. I said, "David, what color are you?" He looked at his bathing suit and said, "I am blue. Today, I am blue." It seemed like a reasonable choice to me.

According to Phinney (1989), David's response was typical of that of many youngsters. He had never been faced with the issues of race (I had forgotten to tell him he was white), and he never gave it much thought.

He did not consider the whole idea important because his family's identity was more involved in issues regarding faith than race.

Later in the fall of that year, David, who loved Superman, explained the difference between the identity he had been taught regarding our faith and the beliefs of his Christian friends. He said, "Marty believes in Superman, but we don't because we're Jewish. Right?" It took me a little longer to explain the finer points of Jewish theology to him. However, ever since he was a very little boy, he had heard me say, "David, you have to be a good, Jewish boy." He is the grandson of a Holocaust survivor; his religion was much more important to us than his color.

Race, like faith, is an issue that has to be taught in order to be internalized and become part of a person's identity. "Race, although it does not exist in the world in any ontologically objective way, it still is real in society (as opposed to nature). Race is a social construction that has real consequences and effects. . . . We know that race is something that is real in society, and that it shapes the way we see ourselves and others. Many rightly claim that race is conceptually unstable. However, this should not lead us to skepticism about race, i.e. that we cannot have any objective knowledge about race. We *can* know what race is and how it works regardless of the various shifts in meaning that have occurred through history and occur geographically" (http://anthropology.net/2008/10/01/race-as-a-social-construct/, p. 1).

Racial identity formation is usually a function of time, place, and culture. The United States has a horrendous history of institutionalized racism toward people of color, especially in the Deep South. However, in other countries, Jews were once considered a race and were treated as outcasts from the broader social community because of the assumed racial failings of the Jewish people.

The meaning of race accepts the idea that race is a marker of status that excludes an individual belonging to a racial minority from the broader society and robs that person of certain powers. Since the dominant culture is accepted as the appropriate marker, others from minority cultures are measured by a standard different from their own; therefore, they are perceived as inferior by virtue of their not meeting the standards created by others who are different from them but who have more power. Race is normally identified through race indicators which are used to indicate each person's race, and consequently what sort of status each individual has in society (http://anthropology.net/2008/10/01/race-as-a social construct/).

In the following lesson plan (table 3.2), students will learn how Scout becomes aware of her race and the power white people had over their black neighbors during the time of the novel. To provide necessary prior knowledge, use the following resources:

- Briggs, J. Views of Race Relations by the 1930's Society of Whites and Blacks. www.pbs.org/wnet/jimcrow/struggle_congress.html.
- *In Their Own Words: A History of the American Negro, 1916–1966*, Milton Meltzer, ed. (New York, 1967), includes documents on post–World War I riots.
- "*Race* in the *1930s*," http://xroads.virginia.edu/~ug02/newyorker/race.html.
- YouTube video: "1930's: The Great Depression, the Dust Bowl, and Racism." (4.26 minutes long)

Once teachers have provided the essential background information, they are ready to implement the following lesson plan.

IDENTITY FORMATION: CLASS

According to Scout, "There was indeed a caste system in Maycomb, but to my mind it worked this way: the old citizens, the present generation of people who had lived side by side for years and years, were utterly predictable to one another" (Lee, 1960, p. 150). However, after Aunt Alexander referred to Walter Cunningham as trash, Jem comes to different conclusions: "I've thought about it a lot lately and I've got it figured out. There's four kinds of folks in the world. There's the ordinary kind like us and the neighbors, there's the kind like the Cunninghams out in the woods, the kind like the Ewells down at the dump, and the Negroes. . . . The thing about it is, our kind of folks don't like the Cunninghams, the Cunninghams don't like the Ewells, and the Ewells hate and despise the colored folks" (p. 259). We can clearly see the developmental differences between Jem and Scout in their understanding of the broader society in which they live.

Table 3.2. Lesson Plan

Lesson Title: Identity Formation and Race
Lesson Unit: *To Kill a Mockingbird (TKAM)*

Lesson Purpose	Racial identity formation.
Essential Question	How do we learn how we are and who we are?
CCSS Standards	**RL. 9–10.1:** Cite strong and thorough textual evidence to support analysis of what the text says explicitly as well as inferences drawn from the text.
Academic CCSS Objectives for Instruction	**RL. 9–10.2:** Determine a theme or central idea of a text and analyze in detail its development over the course of the text, including how it emerges and is shaped and refined by specific details. **RL. 9–10.3:** Analyze how complex characters develop over the course of a text, interact with other characters, and advance the plot or develop the theme. **SL. 9–10.1:** Initiate and participate effectively in a range of collaborative discussions with diverse partners, building on others' ideas and expressing their own clearly and persuasively. **SL. 9–10.1d:** Respond thoughtfully to diverse perspectives, summarize points of agreement and disagreement, and, when warranted, qualify or justify their own views and understandings and make new connections in light of the evidence and reasoning presented.
Habits of Mind Target	"Thinking about your thinking (metacognition). Being aware of your own thoughts, feelings, and actions" (Costa & Kallick, 2009, p. x).
Student Outcome	As a result of today's lesson, students will be able to analyze the process by which Scout and by extension all of us learn about racial identity formation.
Warm up	On your placemat, answer each of the following questions: 1. How did Dr. King's race affect his life? 2. What was Dr. King's goal for racial relationships? 3. How does your race affect your life? 4. How do children develop their racial identity?
Guided Practice	As the teacher, I will model how to find examples from the text that describe and explain how Scout began to develop her own racial identity. On pages 134–137, Scout and Jem visit Calpurnia's church. I will read the pages to the students and model one example of Scout's burgeoning awareness of racial differences.
Independent Practice Time	Each team will be told to find three or four different examples throughout the book of how Scout learns about racial identity from other characters in the novel and her own insights. When each team is finished, they will list the page numbers for each example, and explain how each example is an illustration of racial identity formation.

	Each team will present one of its examples for the class. A prize will be awarded to the team that has done the best job of finding and supporting its example.
Assessment Time	Explain how Lula and Calpurnia demonstrate different facets of racial identity. What does Scout learn from each one?
Habits of Mind (10 points)	Frequently question your students regarding their feelings during this part of the novel. Based on their answers, points should be awarded for the students' ability to recognize their feelings about what is said and done during this part of the novel.
Closure Time	Give an example of how you formed your own racial identity.
Homework	Imagine that the young characters in the novel have grown up. What will Jem be doing twenty years after the novel ended? What will Tom Robinson's oldest son be doing? How will their racial differences affect their adult lives?

According to Erikson (1968), as a youngster, Scout was developing her identity based on class by identifying with Atticus, who was a powerful and important role model who shows Scout what a person of honor and courage can become regardless of class. However, Jem is older and makes his construction of self based on his ability to examine, distinguish between and among groups, and develop his own understanding of the meaning and inferences of their own and others' identities (Phinney, 2000). Although Scout knows that most folks in Maycomb are identified by their family histories and peculiarities, she is not old enough to take into account the differences in tolerance and acceptance accorded to middle-class whites, lower-class whites, white "trash," and blacks.

Although the current literature dealing with class has reframed the traditional stratifications described by Marx, that is, ownership of the means of production and authority (Robinson & Kelley, 1979), even as recently as 2012, teachers in an upper-class setting "provided instruction that gave their students more access to higher status knowledge than did the teachers in the two lower class settings" (DeWitt, 2007, abstract).

Therefore, if class is defined by access to power and authority or on a system based on education and occupational status (Robinson & Kelley,

1979), we are looking at a sociological construct that has far-reaching implications, even today. In order to help students develop a more mature understanding of the role of class in identity formation, teachers should please try the following lesson plan (table 3.3).

Table 3.3. Lesson Plan

Lesson Title: Identity Formation and Class
Lesson Unit: *To Kill a Mockingbird (TKAM)*

Lesson Purpose	Identity formation based on class
Essential Question	How do we learn how we are and who we are?
CCSS Standards **Academic CCSS Objectives for Instruction**	**RL. 9–10.1:** Cite strong and thorough textual evidence to support analysis of what the text says explicitly as well as inferences drawn from the text. **RL. 9–10.2:** Determine a theme or central idea of a text and analyze in detail its development over the course of the text, including how it emerges and is shaped and refined by specific details. **RL. 9–10.3:** Analyze how complex characters develop over the course of a text, interact with other characters, and advance the plot or develop the theme. **SL. 9–10.1:** Initiate and participate effectively in a range of collaborative discussions with diverse partners, building on others' ideas and expressing their own clearly and persuasively. **SL. 9–10.1d:** Respond thoughtfully to diverse perspectives, summarize points of agreement and disagreement, and, when warranted, qualify or justify their own views and understandings and make new connections in light of the evidence and reasoning presented.
Habits of Mind Target	"Thinking about your thinking (metacognition). Being aware of your own thoughts, feelings, and actions" (Costa & Kallick, 2009, p. x).
Student Outcome	As a result of today's lesson, students will be able to analyze the process by which Scout and by extension all of us learn about identity formation based on class.
Warm up	The class will be divided into random groups of four. Each group will be assigned a social class: upper class (Judge Tate), middle class (Finch family), working poor (Cunningham family), hard-core poverty (Ewell family). From the perspective of members of the designated class, students will answer the sample interview statements: I will answer each of the interview statements from my own middle-class perspective. Each team will answer one question from its class status.

Guided Practice	Using an interview questionnaire, each group will answer the questions from their group's class using the following scale: 1= Very true about me; 2= Usually true about me; 3= Rarely true about me, and 4= Not at all true about me. I will answer the interview questions based on my own life experiences.
Independent Practice Time	Each team will arrive at one score for each question. When the scores have been reviewed, the students will discuss their perceived differences based on class and evaluate the results in terms of implications during the time of the novel and today.
Assessment Time	How does Scout develop her final understanding that folks are folks?
Habits of Mind (10 points)	Using informal assessment tools, be sure to monitor how well your students are able to see the problem from another person's perspective and remain aware of their own thinking and feelings at the same time.
Closure Time	What did you learn today that surprised you?
Homework	Ask an adult in your life about class differences when he or she was growing up. Report on the differences between that experience and your own.

Sample Interview Statements

1. You eat dinner with your whole family at least once a week.
2. People come to your home to clean, work on the garden, and do other jobs for your family.
3. Everyone in your family curses freely almost everywhere.
4. Your parents read to you often when you were a young child.
5. Your parents read a lot, and there are many books in your home.
6. You have strong ties to your religion.
7. No one pays attention to where you go at night.
8. There is no scheduled meal time, everyone eats when they get hungry.
9. You are expected to go to college.
10. You have been taught to treat others with respect, especially those in authority.
11. Teachers treat you with respect and courtesy.
12. One or both of your parents dropped out of school.

To people who are very class conscious, there are many clear indicators of a person's status in society based on class. Language, clothing, hair styles, and access to privilege are easily identifiable. However, it is through reading this novel that teachers can hope to help their students to understand the importance of treating everyone with courtesy and respect, regardless of race and class.

Personal Reflections Prior to Teaching This Lesson

I am especially interested in learning how skilled the students will be at identifying class differences accurately. They may not be aware of how much their class contributes to their lifestyles, the expectations placed on them, and their own expectations for the future.

In this as in all lessons, the RI targets are assessed using the in-class formative assessment. However, the speaking and listening and Habits of Mind goals are assessed informally during class discussions and team work. Teachers should keep an ongoing chart that measures students' progress at developing the targeted skills. Progress should always be tracked and evaluated.

IDENTITY FORMATION: GENDER

Throughout the novel, Scout is reprimanded repeatedly by Atticus' sister, Aunt Alexandra, for not displaying the appropriate attitudes and behaviors expected of little girls. In addition to Aunt Alexandra's nagging, Scout is confronted by other attacks regarding gender from other sources of authority. For example, when she attended Calpurnia's church with Jem, she listened attentively to Reverend Sykes. "His sermon was a forthright denunciation of sin . . . he warned his flock against the evils of heady brews, gambling and strange women. Bootleggers caused enough trouble in the Quarters, but women were worse. Again, as I had often met it in my own church, I was confronted with the Impurity of Women doctrine that seemed to preoccupy all clergymen" (Lee, 1960, p. 138). Before Scout is even old enough to understand the innuendo of these comments, she is told that there is something inherently wrong with women.

Even the semi-heroic Calpurnia advises Scout against standing up for what she knows and who she is. After listening to Calpurnia speak in a black dialect, Scout confronts her on her behavior. Cal explains "It's not necessary to tell all you know. It's not ladylike" (p. 143).

It is in this confusing world of expectations that Scout learns that her gender creates burdens and restrictions in the broader community. She can never serve on a jury. Sadly, even Atticus agrees with that policy. He explained his position to Scout and Jem by saying he thought the policy protected women from sordid cases, and besides, "I doubt if we'd ever get a complete case tried—the ladies'd be interrupting to ask questions" (p. 253). Because Atticus believed women lack the capacity to restrain themselves on a jury, Scout internalized this belief and added it to her knowledge of gender expectations and limitations.

Scout is learning she can never express herself freely without being considered un-ladylike; she is always under some cloud of suspicion if she ventures out of the conventions of her gender and culture. According to recent gender development literature, she is being shaped by a series of norms that are a function of time and place, not biology. Nonetheless, the final outcome for Scout and her future sisters has been disastrous. According to Domhoff (2012) 20 percent of the people in the United States own 85 percent of the wealth, and that leaves only 15 percent for wage and salaried workers. Of that population, women and children account for 77 percent of those who live on or below the poverty line.

Some students may not understand the restrictions that Scout lived with and those that still exist, without substantial scaffolding. First, buy several cards typically sent to new parents when their babies are born. Ask the students working in their teams if they can see any differences in the messages sent for little boys vs. little girls. The differences expressed at birth are somewhat stable over time.

Students need to recognize that part of Scout's life, and by extension, their own, is based on gender roles and expectations. The following list of awards (table 3.4) was given at a prestigious private school in the 1990s. Please have a copy of it available for every team when the following lesson plan (table 3.5) is implemented.

Personal Reflection

Before I provide the lesson plan that will help your students understand the role of gender identification, I want to share another story

Table 3.4. Chart of Kindergarten Awards

BOYS' AWARDS	*GIRLS' AWARDS*
Very Best Thinker	*All-around Sweetheart*
Most Eager Learner	*Sweetest Personality*
Most Imaginative	*Cutest Personality*
Most Enthusiastic	*Best Sharer*
Most Scientific	*Best Artist*
Best Friend	*Biggest Heart*
Mr. Personality	*Best Manners*
Hardest Worker	*Best Helper*
Best Sense of Humor	*Most Creative*

with you. When I planned to use this list with my students, I asked one of my senior aides to type up the list for me. Calvin, a wonderful young African-American student, kept showing me the list, which included some intriguing spelling errors which he had made. Every time he showed me the list, I grew angrier. It was clear that I was not angry at Calvin since he was doing his best and doing me a big favor. The list was a real trigger for me, but Calvin could not understand why. Finally, I said, "Calvin, pretend the girls' list read African-Americans and the boys' list said whites." Calvin read the list again, and this time he got furious. "Mrs. Porton, that's wrong!" I said, "Now you know how I feel."

Putting It All Together

The three major issues of the novel are as follows: (1) Why is it a sin to kill a mockingbird? (2) What is the real definition of courage? Honor? (3) How do we really learn to understand another person? When we pair each of these themes with the subtext of the novel, the relationships between the themes and the subtext can be easily seen. The students will be given the opportunity to demonstrate their understanding of the connections between the major themes and the subtext on identity in their writing assignment.

Table 3.5. Lesson Plans

Lesson Title: Identity Formation and Gender
Lesson Unit: *To Kill a Mockingbird* (*TKAM*)

Lesson Purpose	Identity formation based on gender
Essential Question	How do we learn how we are and who we are?
CCSS Standards **Academic CCSS Objectives for Instruction**	**RL. 9–10.1:** Cite strong and thorough textual evidence to support analysis of what the text says explicitly as well as inferences drawn from the text. **RL. 9–10.2:** Determine a theme or central idea of a text and analyze in detail its development over the course of the text, including how it emerges and is shaped and refined by specific details. **RL. 9–10.3:** Analyze how complex characters develop over the course of a text, interact with other characters, and advance the plot or develop the theme. **SL. 9–10.1:** Initiate and participate effectively in a range of collaborative discussions with diverse partners, building on others' ideas and expressing their own clearly and persuasively. **SL.9–10.1d:** Respond thoughtfully to diverse perspectives, summarize points of agreement and disagreement, and, when warranted, qualify or justify their own views and understandings and make new connections in light of the evidence and reasoning presented.
Habits of Mind Target	"Creating, imagining and innovating. Generating new and novel ideas, originality" (Costa & Kallick, 2009, p. x).
Student Outcome	As a result of today's lesson, students will be able to analyze the process by which Scout and by extension all of us learn about identity formation based on gender.
Warm up	Each team will be given the list of kindergarten awards provided above. As a team, the students must identify at least five inequities for both boys and girls illustrated on the list. The team that comes up with the most compelling issues will be awarded a prize.
Guided Practice	We are going to imagine that Scout, Burris Ewell, Walter Cunningham, and Tom Robinson's son are lost in the woods together. Don't let the students dwell on how unlikely that is to happen—we are using our imaginations today! The four kids have to find food and shelter, and create a plan to find their way home. During this exercise, the students will have to imagine who did what, why, and how, as well as how each person's issue (race, class, and gender) affected what each one could and could not do.

(continued)

Table 3.5. *(Continued)*

Independent Practice Time	Our little group is totally lost. It is getting dark, and they are all hungry, tired, and frightened. Someone has to do each of the following tasks. Make your selection of task and character and explain each of your decisions. Peace maker Food finder Shelter creator Trail blazer (who can find their way home).
Assessment Time	On your own, tell the story of this incident from Scout's point of view. Be very specific!
Habits of Mind Assessment	Students' willingness to be creative and accurate in terms of characters' perceptions will be evaluated informally during class work.
Closure Time	What made this task challenging for you? For the characters?
Homework	Write a diary entry from the point of view of Walter Cunningham or Tom's son.

WRITING TO BE INFORMED

Scout encounters Atticus' first and only discussion of sin when owning a gun became a hot topic at the Finch's dinner table. Atticus explains the rules by which he was raised regarding guns. According to Atticus' daddy, he could shoot at any blue jays or other birds if he could hit them, but it was a sin to kill a mockingbird because they don't nest in corn cribs, they don't eat people's crops, they don't do anything but sing beautiful songs for people to hear.

At the end of the novel, when Sherriff Tate and Atticus discuss leaving Boo out of the story of Bob Ewell's death, it was Scout who made the connection between killing an innocent bird and exposing Boo with his shy ways to the limelight. Because she was able to develop a deeper sense of the injustices done to people of color in the Deep South, she understood that hurting anyone simply because that person is vulnerable is a sin.

Boo Radley was as isolated and misunderstood as the blacks who lived in Maycomb. Unable to protect and defend themselves from the more powerful broader community, they were exquisitely well represented by the symbol of the mockingbird. This discussion is a model for the essay the students will be writing, which will require them to make connections between the themes and the subtext of the novel.

For the writing to inform part of the unit (tables 3.6–3.8), the following CCSS Writing Standards will be used:

W. 9–10.2: Write explanatory texts to examine and convey complex ideas, concepts, and information clearly and accurately through the effective selection, organization, and analysis of content.
W. 9–10.2b: Develop the topic with well-chosen, relevant, and sufficient facts, extended definitions, and quotations.
W. 9–10.2c: Use appropriate and varied transitions to link the major sections of the text, and clarify the relationships among complex ideas.
W. 9–10.2f: Provide a concluding statement that follows and supports the information presented.
L. 9–10.2: Demonstrate command of the conventions of standard English capitalization, punctuation, and spelling when writing.

Depending on the strengths and challenges of students' writing skills, teachers might want to make each of the writing targets a separate lesson plan. In addition, teachers can focus on each of the conventions of standard English in separate lesson plans and expect to see improved mastery from the first to the last area of concentration. The summative assessment, of course, will be the students' final draft and should demonstrate mastery of all the writing and language skills.

However, just as in writing arguments, writing to inform includes several discrete skills that students may need extra scaffolding to obtain. A few models of lesson plans that could be used with this writing assignment will be provided. Teachers can supplement with additional plans or delete those that students do not need. In this, as in all my other suggestions, teacher judgment trumps my suggestions!

Based on the results of today's assessments, teachers may be ready to move on to the next skill or they might need to create different lesson plans that address the same skills. Teachers should not move on until all students demonstrate mastery on these skills since they are prerequisite skills for the next steps in this unit.

Table 3.6. Lesson Plan: Writing to Inform

Lesson Title: Making Connections
Lesson Unit: *To Kill a Mockingbird* (*TKAM*)

Lesson Purpose	The writing will demonstrate the use of well-chosen, relevant, and sufficient facts, extended definitions, and quotations to support claims being made.
Essential Question	How do we learn how and who we are?
CCSS Standards	**W. 9–10.2:** Write explanatory texts to examine and convey complex ideas, concepts, and information clearly and accurately through the effective selection, organization, and analysis of content. **W. 9–10.2b:** Develop the topic with well-chosen, relevant, and sufficient facts, extended definitions, and quotations. **L. 9–10.2:** Demonstrate command of the conventions of standard English by following all the rules for capitalization.
LDC Template	Atticus defined courage for Jem and Scout. He said: "It's when you know you're licked before you begin but you begin anyway and you see it through no matter what. You rarely win, but sometimes you do" (Lee, 1960, p. 128). Based on what you have learned about identity formation, find characters that differ in race, class, and gender who fit Atticus' definition of courage. Be sure to supply evidence from the novel to support each of your choices.
Habits of Mind Target	"Thinking and communicating with clarity and precision" (Costa & Kallick, 2009, p. x).
Student Outcome	As a result of participating in today's lesson, students will be able to identify three important characters in the novel who demonstrate Atticus' definition of courage and categorize each of the characters by race, class, and gender.
Materials Needed	Text Notes on identity formation—race, class, and gender
Warm up	Select a character who represents either race, class, and gender who demonstrates courage according to Atticus' definition. For each character, provide the following: Name — Identity — Example of courage Calpurnia — Race — Stood up to Lula
Motivation	Atticus does not think he showed courage when he shot the dog. Do you agree? Why? Why not?
Guided Practice	Calpurnia is one character who displayed courage throughout the novel. She could be a representative of race or gender. In the part of the novel when she protected the children from Lula at church (p. 128), she fit Atticus' definition of courage. I would select her as an example of courage + race. I will use the following sentences as a model for how to introduce the topic and start my first example: Atticus Finch is the true hero of the novel *To Kill a Mockingbird* by Harper Lee. It is his definition of courage that gives the story its moral framework. However, he is not the only courageous

	character in the story. As a result of studying the subtext of the novel as well as its dominant themes, I will provide an example of a character that shows courage based on the three features of identity formation we have examined: race, class, and gender. Calpurnia, the Finch's housekeeper, is an excellent example of a person from a racial minority in the Deep South who shows courage and honor throughout the text.
Independent Practice	Select a representative of gender, race, and class who showed courage. Find evidence in the book (use page numbers) to support your decisions.
Assessment (15 points—10 for clarity of expression and 5 for capitalization)	Write an explanation of why the character you have selected based on gender fits the criteria for showing courage.
Habits of Mind Assessment (10 points)	Team work and class discussions will be evaluated for clarity of thinking. The formative assessment will demonstrate clarity of written expression.
Closure	Atticus is a man of honor and courage. Do you know anyone who is like that in real life? Explain.

Table 3.7. Lesson Plan: Writing to Inform

Lesson Title: Creating Effective Transitions
Lesson Unit: *To Kill a Mockingbird* (*TKAM*)

Lesson Purpose **Essential Question**	Creating effective transitions between ideas. How do we learn how and who we are?
CCSS Standards	**W. 9–10.2**: Write explanatory texts to examine and convey complex ideas, concepts, and information clearly and accurately through the effective selection, organization, and analysis of content. **W. 9–10.2c:** Use appropriate and varied transitions to link the major sections of the text, and clarify the relationships among complex ideas. **L. 9–10.2**: Demonstrate command of the conventions of standard English by following all the rules for spelling.
LDC Template	Atticus defined courage for Jem and Scout. He said: "It's when you know you're licked before you begin but you begin anyway and you see it through no matter what. You rarely win, but sometimes you do" (Lee, 1960, p. 128). Based on what you have learned about identity formation, find characters that differ in race, class, and gender who fit Atticus' definition of courage. Be sure to supply evidence from the novel to support each of your choices.

(continued)

Table 3.7. *(Continued)*

Habits of Mind Target	"Thinking and communicating with clarity and precision" (Costa & Kallick, 2009, p. x).
Student Outcome	As a result of today's lesson, students will be able to write effective transitions between the three examples of identity formation and courage.
Materials Needed	Text Notes on identity formation—race, class, and gender
Warm up	I will tell a story without transitions. Each team will have to guess at the relationships that exist among the parts of the story. The team that does the best job at making sense of the story will win a prize.
Motivation	Why are transitions important? What do they add to a story, text, or anecdote?
Guided Practice	I will use the model of the connection between the theme that deals with the sin inherent in killing a mockingbird and Scout's understanding of its application to cruelty to the vulnerable members of society. I will create a model of the transition needed between my first and my next example. Model: Although Scout's perceptions about Boo Radley and the sin of killing a mockingbird are very insightful, this link is not unique. The mockingbird also represents all of those who are vulnerable as a result of race, class, and gender.
Independent Practice	Write a transition sentence(s) between your first example and your next. Be sure to demonstrate the relationship between the two.
Assessment (15 points—10 for clarity of expression and 5 for spelling)	Create a transition sentence between these two ideas: Killing a mockingbird is a symbol of cruelty to innocent creatures. Tom Robinson represents a person who is vulnerable to cruelty because of his race.
Habits of Mind Assessment (10 points)	Team work and class discussions will be evaluated for clarity of thinking. The formative assessment will demonstrate clarity of written expression.
Closure	Why are transitions essential to good writing?

Even though the CCSS strands require higher-order thinking skills, they are not out of reach of struggling learners. If teachers break down the targets into manageable chunks and provide all of the scaffolding their students will need, any student who has sufficient cognitive strengths should be able to master the skills required by CCSS.

In the writing unit we covered regarding Dr. King's letter, students were not asked to work on strong concluding statements because mastering claims, evidence, and warrants was sufficient for any unit. However, this unit (table 3.8) provides the opportunity for students to learn how to draw their essay to a meaningful close.

POINTS TO PONDER

We are taking a quantum leap of faith by expecting struggling learners placed in high school English classes to manage the complex and sophisticated nuances of a classic American novel. However, it is clear that, with the appropriate scaffolding, high-interest topics, and meaningful and varied opportunities for students to participate in higher-order thinking skill activities, this is a reasonable expectation for every student.

REFLECTIONS

To Kill a Mockingbird is a deceptively easy novel to read. However, it has become an American classic because its themes are universal and its characters credible. The essential conflicts of the novel are readily apparent, but it takes a close read to become sensitive to all its nuances. For this reason, this novel is a natural selection for classes with discouraged learners. On your own or with a partner, respond to the following:

1. Why is it necessary to connect any reading to students' lives?
2. How do sociological issues affect your content?
3. Think of your next unit and break it down into its major components. How many and what kind of lesson plans will you need?
4. How will you connect your content with struggling learners?
5. How is it possible to bridge the gap between struggling learners and CCSS?

Table 3.8. Lesson Plan: Writing to Inform

Lesson Title: Creating a Meaningful Conclusion
Lesson Unit: *To Kill a Mockingbird* (*TKAM*)

Lesson Purpose	Creating meaningful concluding statements.
Essential Question	How do we learn how and who we are?
CCSS Standards	**W. 9–10.2**: Write explanatory texts to examine and convey complex ideas, concepts, and information clearly and accurately through the effective selection, organization, and analysis of content. **W. 9–10.2f:** Provide a concluding statement that follows and supports the information presented. **L. 9–10.2**: Demonstrate command of the conventions of standard English by following all the rules for punctuation.
LDC Template	Atticus defined courage for Jem and Scout. He said: "It's when you know you're licked before you begin but you begin anyway and you see it through no matter what. You rarely win, but sometimes you do" (Lee, 1960, p. 128). Based on what you have learned about identity formation, find characters that differ in race, class, and gender who fit Atticus' definition of courage. Be sure to supply evidence from the novel to support each of your choices.
Habits of Mind Target	"Thinking and communicating with clarity and precision" (Costa & Kallick, 2009, p. x).
Student Outcome	As a result of today's lesson, students will be able to write a meaningful conclusion that draws the key ideas together and supports the main ideas of the essay.
Materials Needed	Text Notes on identity formation—race, class, and gender
Warm up	I will read pp. 321–323 to the class. Students will draw, act out, or put the ending scene in their own words.
Motivation	Why is the conclusion of the novel so effective and meaningful? What conclusions can we draw from the end of this novel?
Guided Practice	Make a list of the three examples you have written about for your essay. What is the fundamental lesson that each one tells? What do you want your readers to remember about your essay?
Independent Practice	Write one or two concluding sentences for your essay. Be sure they draw the essay to a close, include the main ideas you discussed, and leave your reader with a clear idea of the purpose of the essay.
Assessment (15 points for clarity of expression)	Review the conclusion written by one member of your team. Check to see if it contains all of the required elements. Make specific comments that will help your writer improve the first draft.
Habits of Mind Assessment (10 points)	Team work and class discussions will be evaluated for clarity of thinking. The formative assessment will demonstrate clarity of written expression.
Closure	How do good conclusions make any writing more significant?

REFERENCES

Common Core State Standards Initiative (2012). www.corestandards.org.

Costa, A. L., & Kallick, B. (2009). *Habits of mind across the curriculum*. Alexandria, VA: ASCD.

DeWitt, S. W. (2007). Dividing the digital divide: Instructional use of computers in social studies. *Theories & Research in Social Education, 35*(2).

Domhoff, G. W. (2012). www2.ucsc.edu/whorulesamerica/power/wealth.html.

Erikson, E. (1959). *Identity and the life cycle*. New York: International Universities Press.

Erikson, E. (1968). *Identity: Youth and crisis*. New York: Norton.

Flum, H., & Kaplan, A. (2012). Identity formation in educational settings: A contextualized view of theory and research in practice. *Contemporary Educational Psychology, 37*, 240–245.

http://anthropology.net/2008/10/01/race-as-a-social-construct/.

Jones, S. J. (1997). *Identity and communication in cyber society*. Thousand Oaks, CA: Sage.

Lee, H. (1960). *To kill a mockingbird*. New York: HarperCollins.

McEwen, M. K. (2003). The nature and use of theory. In S. R. Komives & D. B. Woodard Jr. (Eds.), *Student services: A handbook for the profession* (4th ed., 153–178). San Francisco: Jossey-Bass.

Muuss, R. E. (1996). *Theories of adolescence* (6th ed.) New York: McGraw Hill.

Phinney, J. S. (1989). Stages of ethnic development in minority and group adolescents. *Journal of Early Adolescence, 9*, 34–39.

Phinney, J. S. (2000). Identity formation across cultures: The interaction of personal, societal, and historical change. *Human Development, 43*, 27–31.

Robinson, R. V., & Kelley, J. (1979). Class as conceived by Marx and Dahrendorf: Effects income inequality and politics in the United States and Great Britain. *American Sociological Review, 44* (February): 38–58.

Sinai, M., Kaplan, A., & Flum, H. (2012). Promoting identity exploration within the school curriculum: A design-based study in a junior high literature lesson in Israel. *Contemporary Educational Psychology, 37*, 195–205.

Torres, V. (2003). Influences on ethnic identity development of Latino college students in the first two years of college. *Journal of College Student Development, 44*, 532–547.

Torres, V., Jones, S. R., & Renn, K. A. (2009). Identity development theories in student affairs: Origins, current status, and new approaches. *Journal of College Student Development, 50*, 577–596.

Weber, L. (1998). A conceptual framework for understanding race, class, gender, and sexuality. *Psychology of Women Quarterly, 22*, 13–22.

4

HOW DOES A MORAL PERSON MAKE DECISIONS IN AN IMMORAL WORLD?

> In matters of truth and justice, there is no difference between large and small problems, for issues concerning the treatment of people are all the same.
>
> —Albert Einstein

In this chapter, we will be reading Simon Wiesenthal's (1969) *The Sunflower*, which is the personal story of his life, as a Jew, in the concentration camps during World War II. This particular account describes one of Wiesenthal's experiences near the end of the war. It brings into specific focus the ethical dilemmas that moral people living in an immoral world must face.

By the time most students have reached tenth grade, they are ready to tackle some of the harshest realities in life as long as they are learning in a safe and caring environment. However, students will need to know the following in order to appreciate the circumstances surrounding this text.

In 1939, Germany and Russia signed a "non-aggression" pact and agreed to divide Poland between them. Shortly after that the Russian army began the "Red purge of Jewish merchants, factory owners and other professionals" (www.museumoftolerance.com, p. 1). This was not a new activity for the Russians, as they had a long, vile history of persecuting Jews long before World War II began.

Simon Wiesenthal and his family became victims of the purge. His stepfather was arrested and died in prison; his stepbrother was shot. He was sent to work in a factory and managed to keep himself, his wife, and his mother relatively safe until 1942. By the end of August 1942, his mother was sent to a death camp, and by the end of that year, a total of eighty-nine members of Wiesenthal and his wife's family had been murdered by the Nazi regime. Wiesenthal was sent to a death camp, but was able to escape. He was recaptured and sent back, but in 1944, Germany's eastern front was collapsing and one of the guards at the death camp chose to keep Wiesenthal and a few other remaining prisoners alive (www.museumoftolerance.com).

After the liberation, most of the survivors spent a great deal of time recovering from their illnesses and wounds. Even before Wiesenthal had recovered, he made it his life's work to prepare evidence of the German atrocities during World War II. He sought out escaped SS guards, leaders of the Reich, and any other willing members of the Nazi regime.

His most publicized capture was Adolf Eichmann, who supervised the implementation of the Final Solution (the murder of all the Jews in Europe). With Wiesenthal's help, Eichmann was captured by Israeli agents, deported to Israel, and executed in Israel on May 31, 1961. The capture of Eichmann is well documented in both text and film, and it is a dramatic story.

Wiesenthal wrote his book, *The Sunflower*, which was published in 1969. This book describes a horrific incident during World War II. The story is told from Wiesenthal's first-person involved point of view. Following the narrative, Wiesenthal asked a wide-ranging panel of distinguished scholars, religious leaders, political leaders, and others to respond to the decision he had made.

Not all of the experts agree with Wiesenthal's decision, but their reasoning provides insights into the various supportable moral-decision-making processes students need to be exposed to at this point in their lives. References from Holocaust deniers are not recommended during this unit, as their position is morally and historically indefensible.

Every student will read Book One: *The Sunflower*, in order to know and understand the event. Responses provided in the part of the text Wiesenthal named "The Symposium" will be divided among the teams so that each team can analyze one of four different perspectives, make individual decisions, and participate in class discussions that focus on how a moral person makes decisions in an immoral world.

On a Personal Note

I am the daughter-in-law of a Holocaust survivor. My mother-in-law, Bertha, of blessed memory, lived on a large farm her family owned in Czechoslovakia. Her father employed many of their Christian neighbors, and according to Bertha, they lived together in peace and harmony until the Nazi invasion.

Bertha's parents were able to send two of their youngest daughters to live with Christian neighbors; the girls, who were raised in a very observant Jewish family, were told to say they were Christians in order to survive. Her brother was conscripted into the army. Her parents were murdered soon after the invasion. Bertha, her husband, and their two small children hid in the forest until, after having handed over their last bit of jewelry to neighbors in return for not exposing them, the neighbors took their jewels and immediately told the Nazis where the family was hiding.

My father-in-law was taken away from his family and shot during one of the long marches. Bertha and her two sons were taken on a cattle car to Bergen-Belsen. Fortunately, they were not captured until close to the end of the war, and they were alive when the liberators entered the camps.

When the liberation came, the soldiers saw the condition of the surviving prisoners and started imposing their own justice on the guards. Bertha said, "My friends came to tell me that the soldiers were hanging the prison guards. 'Come watch.' I said, 'No, I have seen enough killings. I don't want to watch anyone else die.'" I often wonder what Bertha would have said to Wiesenthal regarding the decision he made. She was one of the finest people I have ever had the privilege to know, and this book is dedicated, in part, to her memory.

I tell you this story so that you will understand my position and my passion regarding this topic. I truly believe that if this text does not move you, you should teach something else, such as Wiesel's (1958) Night.

IN THIS CHAPTER

In this chapter, strategies for helping students gain a better understanding of this time in history through a literary lens, develop an appreciation of the writer's craft, and experience a more refined view of the complexity and confusion of trying to make moral decisions in an immoral world will be provided. This is not a theoretical discussion for students. Many live in gang-infested neighborhoods where life expectancy is short, violence is pervasive, and loyalties are questionable.

COMMON CORE STATE STANDARDS AND *THE SUNFLOWER*

For these purposes, attention will be paid to the following Common Core State Standards:

RI. 9–10.1: Cite strong and thorough textual evidence to support analysis of what the text says explicitly as well as inferences drawn from the text.

RI. 9–10.4: Determine the meaning of words and phrases as they are used in a text, including figurative, connotative, and technical meanings.

RI. 9–10.5: Analyze in detail how an author's ideas or claims are developed and refined by larger portions of the text.

RI. 9–10.6: Determine an author's point of view or purpose in a text and analyze how an author uses rhetoric to advance that point of view or purpose.

W. 9–10.1: Write arguments to support claims in an analysis of substantive topics, using valid reasoning, and relevant and sufficient evidence.

W.9–10.1a: Introduce precise claims, distinguish the claims from alternate or opposing claims, and create an organization that establishes clear relationships among claims, counterclaims, reasons, and evidence.

W. 9–10.1e: Provide a concluding section that follows from and supports the argument presented.

SL. 9–10.3: Evaluate a speaker's point of view, reasoning, and use of evidence and rhetoric, identifying any fallacious reasoning or exaggerated or distorted evidence.

SL. 9–10.1: Initiate and participate effectively in a range of collaborative discussions with diverse partners, building on others' ideas and expressing their own clearly and persuasively.

SL. 9–10.1d: Respond thoughtfully to diverse perspectives, summarize points of agreement and disagreement, and, when warranted, qualify or justify their own views and understanding and make new connections in light of the evidence and reasoning presented.

L. 9–10.1b: Use various types of phrases to convey specific meanings and add variety and interest to writing.

ORGANIZATIONAL STRUCTURE OF THIS CHAPTER

We will begin with the scaffolding students need before they start to read the text. Various vocabulary strategies will be discussed, and specific lesson plans (tables 4.1–4.3) will be provided. The plans will cover Wiesenthal's story before he met the dying soldier, the soldier's story, and Wiesenthal's choices at the end of the war. In addition, four of the responses to Wiesenthal's last question have been selected for the students to read. Each team will be given one of the responses to analyze, discuss, and debate. A sample lesson plan will be provided for this section.

Finally, the students will be asked to write an argument supporting their own position on Wiesenthal's question. This is not to be an exercise in expressing opinions; they are expected to research the following topics: morality, forgiveness, atonement, and repentance, before they begin to write. Sample lesson plans for helping students conduct research will be presented.

THE SUNFLOWER

Before teachers begin teaching the text, they should share any or all of the following websites with their students:

1. www.museumoftolerance.com. This site is dedicated to the memory and the work of Simon Wiesenthal.
2. www1.yadvashem.org/yv/en/holocaust/index.asp. From this site, go to Holocaust History Museum and choose "virtual tour" or enter any of the gates described on the home page.
3. www.holocaustsurvivors.org.
4. www.holocaust-history.org.
5. www.history.com/topics/the-holocaust.

Table 4.1. Lesson Plan

Lesson Title: Life in the Camps
Lesson Unit: *The Sunflower*

Lesson Purpose	Recognizing the importance of perspective.
Essential Question	How does a moral person make moral decisions in an immoral world?
CCSS Standards **Academic CCSS Objectives for Instruction**	**RI. 9–10.1:** Cite strong and thorough textual evidence to support analysis of what the text says explicitly as well as inferences drawn from the text. **RI. 9–10.4:** Determine the meaning of words and phrases as they are used in a text, including figurative, connotative, and technical meanings. **RI. 9–10.6:** Determine an author's point of view or purpose in a text and analyze how an author uses rhetoric to advance that point of view or purpose. **SL. 9–10.3:** Evaluate a speaker's point of view, reasoning, and use of evidence and rhetoric, identifying any fallacious reasoning or exaggerated or distorted evidence. **SL. 9–10.1:** Initiate and participate effectively in a range of collaborative discussions with diverse partners, building on others' ideas and expressing their own clearly and persuasively. **SL. 9–10.1d:** Respond thoughtfully to diverse perspectives, summarize points of agreement and disagreement, and, when warranted, qualify or justify their own views and understandings and make new connections in light of the evidence and reasoning presented.
Essential Question	How does a moral person make decisions in an immoral world?
Habits of Mind Target	"Remaining open to continuous learning" (Costa & Kallick, 2009, p. x).
Student Outcomes	As a result of participating in this lesson, students will describe during class discussions and in written work their understandings of how each person's perspective affects how any situation is experienced and explained.
Warm up	Answer the following questions based on the videos we have seen: 1. What was the Holocaust? 2. Where did it happen? 3. Why did it happen? 4. Could it happen in the United States?
Guided Practice Time	Ask every student in your class to stand. Tell them when the group with which they are identified is called, they have to sit down: Jews Jehovah's witnesses Those with serious physical challenges Any child of color

	When all of the classifications have been called, ask the students who are sitting whether the students who are still standing have more right to live than they do.
Independent Practice Time	Read pp. 3–9 (stop at "what I had long felt to be true"). Guide question—Read to find out about Simon's life in the camps. As a team, answer the following questions: 1. Describe the story teller. 2. Who was with him? 3. Why was he in there? 4. How has he changed since before his capture? Before the students read, divide the following terms into four groups. Each team is responsible for looking up its own word and sharing the meaning of the word with the whole class when they come to the word in their reading. p. 5: insinuations polyglot p. 7: platitudes commandant p. 9: savoring Read pp. 9–15 (stop at "my dreadful tomb"). Guide question—How did the passersby and the German soldiers feel about the Jews? Answer these questions from the point of view of one of the following: Team : SS Officer Team 2: askari Team 3: people of Lemberg Team 4: a fellow student of Wiesenthal's before the war 1. Why were the Jews in prison camps? 2. What will happen to the Jews? Why? 3. Why were the Jews marching? 4. How will the war end? Before the students read these pages, they need to define the following terms: p. 12: mitigated p. 13: desisted Read pp. 15–20 (stop at "Only there wouldn't be a Poland either."). Guide question—What was life like in Poland for the Jews before the war? 1. Describe what happens to you when you get up until you go to your first class. 2. What did the Jewish students experience at the Technical High School? Why? 3. Describe the "day without the Jews." When and why were they held? 4. What did the sunflower represent to Wiesenthal? Read pp. 20–22 (stop at "'Are you a Jew?' She asked."). Guide question—How were the Jews treated during the war?

(continued)

Table 4.1. *(Continued)*

	1. What happened to the Technical High School? 2. How did the soldier look at the prisoners (p. 21)? Why? What does that tell you? 3. What did he call the prisoners? Why? How do you think he felt after he said that? 4. What did the prisoners have to do? Why? Before they start the reading ask the students to predict what the following words will mean. After the reading, make sure everyone has the correct definition p. 21: molested convalescent p. 22: vile stench After each section of the reading, ask the students to supply evidence from their notes on the Holocaust or the text. If there are any weak answers, the other students are expected to point out the problems with the claims being made.
Assessment Time	Each student will respond to this question: What could make one person believe another person is subhuman (higher than an animal but lower than a human being)?
Habits of Mind (10 points)	Using informal assessments, determine if students remain on task, stay focused and alert during the lesson.
Closure Time	Have you ever seen or experienced evil? Explain
Homework	Write five questions about the story from Wiesenthal's point of view.

Teachers certainly do not have to go to all of the sites listed on page 89, but they should definitely see the site at Yad Vashem, which means "a place and a name" in Hebrew (referring to the millions who were not given the dignity of a Jewish burial), and the Museum of Tolerance. Select any of the other sites that will help students gain sufficient understanding of the time in history they will be reading about.

The Dying Soldier's Story

This is a very touching, dramatic, and horrifying section of the text. In it, a dying soldier tells Wiesenthal what he did during the war and asks Wiesenthal, on behalf of the Jewish people, to forgive him. The text must be read with a high degree of fluency. Therefore, it is suggested that if possible the teacher and one strong reader divide the reading between them so that one is the voice of Wiesenthal and the other the dying soldier.

The students need to be reading along while the oral reading is provided. When the reading is complete, give the students a chance to process what they have just read and heard. Therefore, struggling learners will have a better chance of understanding the text.

Before students begin the reading, teachers might want to go to www.holocaustresearchproject.org/holoprelude/hitleryouth.html. This site provides necessary information regarding Hitler Youth, and most students will need to understand the conflict in loyalties that belonging to this group created for its members. For example, the youth were told to report anyone who expressed negative opinions about Hitler to the authorities. Children were encouraged to report on their parents' conversations, their neighbors' activities, and their teachers' attitudes.

If teachers believe their students have the maturity and need to view this video, go to "Behind the Swastika: Nazi Atrocities," available through Google. The footage is very real, but the video was made in 1945 before the full extent of the atrocities had been revealed; nevertheless, it is very explicit.

This section of the text ends on page 75. Teachers should divide the reading into manageable chunks for their students. Teachers need to follow the same format throughout the reading so that the students hear the story clearly and can concentrate on its meaning rather than just decoding difficult text. Teachers must continue to let their at-risk students predict the meaning of the vocabulary terms, as that may lighten the atmosphere of the class while teachers help the students deal with the horrors of the text.

The real goal in this section is to present both sides reasonably and with compassion. If Wiesenthal's decision were easy, he would never have felt compelled to tell this story. It is also suggested that students keep a journal about their reactions to this story and its meaning for them. If the reading does not take the entire class time, teachers can use the journal as the closing activity for the day.

Table 4.2. Lesson Plan

Lesson Title: The Dying Soldier's Story
Lesson Unit: *The Sunflower*

Lesson Purpose	Recognizing the importance of perspective.
Essential Question	How does a moral person make moral decisions in an immoral world?
CCSS Standards **Academic CCSS Objectives for Instruction**	**RI. 9–10.1:** Cite strong and thorough textual evidence to support analysis of what the text says explicitly as well as inferences drawn from the text. **RI. 9–10.4:** Determine the meaning of words and phrases as they are used in a text, including figurative, connotative, and technical meanings. **RI. 9–10.6:** Determine an author's point of view or purpose in a text and analyze how an author uses rhetoric to advance that point of view or purpose. **SL. 9–10.3:** Evaluate a speaker's point of view, reasoning, and use of evidence and rhetoric, identifying any fallacious reasoning or exaggerated or distorted evidence. **SL. 9–10.1:** Initiate and participate effectively in a range of collaborative discussions with diverse partners, building on others' ideas and expressing their own clearly and persuasively. **SL. 9–10.1d:** Respond thoughtfully to diverse perspectives, summarize points of agreement and disagreement, and, when warranted, qualify or justify their own views and understandings and make new connections in light of the evidence and reasoning presented.
Essential Question	How does a moral person make moral decisions in an immoral world?
Student Outcomes	As a result of participating in this lesson, students will describe during class discussions and in written work their understanding of how each person's perspective affects how any situation is experienced and explained.
Habits of Mind Target	"Remaining open to continuous learning" (Costa & Kallick, 2009, p. x).
Warm up	1. Have you ever been a member of a group/club/organization? Why did you join? 2. How does peer pressure affect your decisions? 3. Could you report your parents, friends, or neighbors to the police? Explain. 4. If you do a very bad thing as a member of a group, are you responsible for your behavior? Explain.
Guided Practice Time	The general educator and a strong reader will divide the reading on pp. 22–27. The students need to read along as the teachers read out loud to them. Guide question—What happens to a person when all feeling for others is gone?

	Read pp. 27–33 following the same format. Guide question—Why is the dying soldier anxious to tell his story to Wiesenthal? Before the reading, students will predict the meaning of the following words and check for accuracy when they read the words in the text: p. 27: resigned p. 29: SS p. 30: incurred p. 31: coherency Read pp. 34–43 following the same format. Guide question—How is it possible for a normal person to do something horrible? Before the reading, students will predict the meaning of the following words and check for accuracy when they read the words in the text: p. 35: disavowal p. 36: façade p. 41: automatons p. 42: detonations Stop the reading now. Allow the students to react to the story in their teams, but do not ask them to respond to the whole class for a few minutes so they can process the true story.
Independent Practice Time	This plan does not involve the usual feature of independent practice. However, students are to answer the guide questions in their teams. A whole class discussion regarding the questions will be held before the next phase of the reading begins.
Assessment Time	What did the dying soldier want Wiesenthal to do? Why?
Habits of Mind	Be sure students are reading, processing, and staying focused during the oral reading.
Closure Time	How do you explain evil?

After the Confession

Wiesenthal picks up his narrative two years after the dying soldier's confession. While in the camp, Wiesenthal met a man he came to admire, who had studied for the priesthood. As the two men talk, Wiesenthal recounts his experience with the dying man and asks for his friend's opinion. Perhaps this was the origin of the second half of the text, because Wiesenthal began to consider the decision differently after this exchange.

Table 4.3. Lesson Plan

Lesson Title: The War Comes to an End
Lesson Unit: *The Sunflower*

Lesson Purpose	Recognizing the importance of perspective.
Essential Question	How does a moral person make moral decisions in an immoral world?
CCSS Standards	**RI. 9–10.1:** Cite strong and thorough textual evidence to support analysis of what the text says explicitly as well as inferences drawn from the text. **RI. 9–10.4:** Determine the meaning of words and phrases as they are used in a text, including figurative, connotative, and technical meanings.
Academic CCSS Objectives for Instruction	**RI. 9–10.5:** Analyze in detail how an author's ideas or claims are developed and refined by larger portions of the text. **RI. 9–10.6:** Determine an author's point of view or purpose in a text and analyze how an author uses rhetoric to advance that point of view or purpose. **SL. 9–10.3:** Evaluate a speaker's point of view, reasoning, and use of evidence and rhetoric, identifying any fallacious reasoning or exaggerated or distorted evidence. **SL. 9–10.1:** Initiate and participate effectively in a range of collaborative discussions with diverse partners, building on others' ideas and expressing their own clearly and persuasively. **SL. 9–10.1d:** Respond thoughtfully to diverse perspectives, summarize points of agreement and disagreement, and, when warranted, qualify or justify their own views and understandings and make new connections in light of the evidence and reasoning presented.
Essential Question	How does a moral person make moral decisions in an immoral world?
Habits of Mind Target	"Remaining open to continuous learning" (Costa and Kallick, 2009, p. x).
Student Outcomes	As a result of participating in this lesson, students will describe during class discussions and written work their understanding of how each person's perspective affects how any situation is experienced and explained.
Warm up	1. What are some of the important lessons your friends have taught you? 2. Why is it easier to listen to a peer than a parent? 3. Do you ever feel that no one really understands you? Why? 4. Could you forgive a group of people who had destroyed your family?
Guided Practice Time	Read pp. 78–83 (stop at "each had a better understanding of the other's views."). Guide question—What are some of the major differences between Bolek and Wiesenthal?

	Before the reading, students will predict the meaning of the following words and check for accuracy when they read the words in the text: p. 79: sangfroid p. 80: incessantly tortured p. 31: atheists Read pp. 34–43 following the same format. Guide question—How is it possible for a normal person to do something horrible?
Independent Practice Time	This plan does not involve the usual feature of independent practice. However, students are to answer the guide questions in their teams. A whole class discussion regarding the questions will be held before the next phase of the reading begins.
Assessment Time	How did meeting Bolek affect Wiesenthal?
Habits of Mind (10 points)	Using informal assessment tools, evaluate each student's willingness to remain open to the various points of view expressed in this section.
Closure Time	Can you forgive evil behavior?

In this reading, the students need to be aware that by that time, none of the prisoners expected to live for more than a week. There was no food, and the remaining prisoners were being murdered in even greater numbers as the Nazis realized they were losing the war and did not want any witnesses to their barbarity to survive.

It is very difficult for students who live in relative peace and comfort to empathize with starving, dying men, but they need to get a sense of the time and place of the text. There are two sites on Google that may be helpful. The first one is www.historyplace.com/worldwar2/timeline, which includes pictures of what the Allies found when they entered Buchenwald. The pictures are graphic, but they include a photo of Elie Wiesel, the winner of the Nobel Prize for Peace. The second site has more battle pictures and may be helpful for some students. Go to www.theatlantic.com/infocus/2011/.../world-war-ii...europe/100160/. Both of these sites can help the students visualize the chaos and horror of the war.

In this section of the text, Wiesenthal experiences the ending days of the war and life after the war. He has to try to reconcile the concept of forgiveness with the horrors he has experienced and seen.

Teachers should continue reading the story following this format. The guide questions must be relevant to the text, be probing, and help the students gain a sophisticated understanding of the passages they have just read. Teachers should not go to the next section until the assessment responses indicate that the students have a thorough understanding of the text.

BOOK TWO: "THE SYMPOSIUM"

For this section of the unit, four different responses have been chosen for the class to study. The Dalai Lama (from Tibet, spiritual leader of Buddhists), Cardinal Franz König (archbishop of Vienna), Harold Kushner (American rabbi), and Smail Balić (a leading expert on oriental languages) were among the respected respondents to Wiesenthal's questions; they have been selected because they represent various constituents and faiths around the world.

Since English 10 is normally devoted to the study of world literature, this is an excellent vehicle for teachers to introduce their students to variations in culture and values from all over the world. To help students understand Wiesenthal's decision from a Jewish perspective, the following is a response to Wiesenthal's question:

> Interestingly, it has been pointed out that without exception, every Christian respondent (as well as some representatives of other faiths) felt that Simon was wrong in not forgiving the Nazi murderer, while those who were Jewish believed he was right. It has been suggested that this astonishing fact stems not from man's frail nature, the tendency to side with his own—in this case Jews with their coreligionists and Christians with theirs—but from the fundamentally different teachings of these respective religions. . . .
>
> [According to the Mishnah] For sins against G-d, the Day of Atonement (Yom Kippur) brings forgiveness. For sins against one's neighbor, the Day of Atonement brings no forgiveness until one has become reconciled with one's neighbor.
>
> The real question is not whether or not he should have forgiven, but whether or not he could have: Thus, the real question, overlooked by many of the respondents, is not whether or not Simon should have forgiven the Nazi, but whether or not he could have forgiven him. Per-

haps his response could have been: "I may *want* to (especially given the circumstances) but I simply am not *able* to." (www.chabad.org/article.asp?aid=1010092)

Teachers need to make a copy of this information and share it with the students who will be representing Rabbi Kushner and then the rest of the students after the class conducts its symposium.

The Symposium

First teachers have each team choose one of the names from out of a hat so that the assignments are random. Next, each team has to research the expert whose name they have drawn. Who is he? What has he done? Written? Contributed to society? Why was he chosen to respond to Wiesenthal's question? When teachers are satisfied that each team is knowledgeable about the expert, students should read the person's response and answer the following questions:

1. Does the writer agree or disagree with Wiesenthal?
2. How do you know?
3. What were the writer's claims? Evidence? Warrants?
4. Was the argument sound? Logical? Convincing?

Next teachers have each team create five questions for the symposium. The questions should deal with the essential conflict that Wiesenthal faced, the realities of the treatment of the Jews, the complexity of making moral decisions in an immoral world, and issues surrounding forgiveness.

When all of the preparations have been completed, teachers should ask one student from each team to represent the writer the team has studied. Each speaker will give a brief description of the writer's opinion; explain and justify the writer's claims, evidence, and warrants; and discuss how the team felt about this writer. After each speaker has presented his position, the whole class should participate by using their team's questions, creating questions on the spot based on what the other students have heard and said, and generating questions based on the evidence that has been supplied to the class.

Teachers need to create a rubric for both speakers and audience to measure their ability to evaluate a speaker's point of view, reasoning, and use of evidence and rhetoric. Students are expected to identify any fallacious reasoning or exaggerated or distorted evidence.

The students should be evaluated on their ability to initiate and participate effectively in a collaborative discussion with diverse partners, building on others' ideas and expressing their own clearly and persuasively. The rubric should measure students' ability to respond thoughtfully to diverse perspectives, summarize points of agreement and disagreement, and, when warranted, qualify or justify their own views and understandings and make new connections in light of the evidence and reasoning presented (Common Core State Standards).

WRITING TO PERSUADE

The students have just finished reading a horrifying and true account of one of the darkest chapters in history. This writing assignment is designed to help them filter and digest the degree of cruelty people are capable of and, in contrast, the acts of loving kindness that people can display even in the worst circumstances.

Throughout the account, Wiesenthal tells of incidents when total strangers risked their lives to give food to the concentration camp victims, acts of kindness among the prisoners, and the inevitability of hope. This text not only has the resounding capacity to teach hope and resilience, it provides a perfect vehicle for allowing students in a calm, caring, and thoughtful environment to think about some of the most difficult dilemmas of life: How does a moral person make moral decisions in an immoral world?

Students are not encouraged to write opinion papers, as that task does not require them to assemble, assess, and analyze a variety of sources in order to arrive at well-documented claims, evidence, and warrants. Therefore, the first step in the process includes giving the operative terms to the teams so that each team becomes an expert on the following: morality, forgiveness, atonement, and repentance; each team must research the terms from the point of view of the faith held by the respondent they are studying.

For example, Christian beliefs about atonement are very different from Jewish beliefs. For those groups studying the Cardinal's response, the Christian interpretation should be used. However, the Dalai Lama, Smail Balić, and Rabbi Kushner are not Christian, and the groups that are studying them should use the definitions that are part of the Buddhist, Muslim, and Jewish faiths respectively.

Next, teachers divide the teams so that one person becomes the expert on his team's writer; the rest of the team visits each of the other experts. After every student has had the opportunity to visit one of the other groups, the students regroup and share their new knowledge with the members of their home team. When teachers are satisfied that all of the students have a working knowledge of the four writers and terms selected, they are ready to implement the following lesson plan (table 4.4).

The next steps for writing the argument include helping the students create a five-paragraph response to the prompt: (1) thesis, (2) claims, evidence, and warrants supporting the writer's position, (3) how the concepts of morality, forgiveness, atonement, and repentance affect the writer's decision, (4) explaining and accounting for the opposing view, (5) conclusion.

Each lesson plan should be devoted to developing a coherent, evidence-based argument. Since one of the Core standards deals with language skills, the next lesson plan (table 4.5) provided will describe effective strategies for improving students' writing skills, specifically the use of phrases and clauses to add variety and additional information to the students' writing. It is up to teachers to decide when they want to use this plan, but students' work should be evaluated on their use of phrases and clauses during this writing unit.

Effective Strategies for Teaching Grammar

Don and Jenny Killgallon (2007) created a superb system for teaching grammar that actually generalizes from exercises to students' writing. For these purposes, one lesson plan for teaching appositives will be provided, although there are many other useful phrases and clauses that need to be included.

Appositives are not needed for the sentence to express a complete thought, but using them adds interesting details and style to the writing.

According to Killgallon and Killgallon (2007), an appositive always answers one of the following questions:

> Who is he? Who is she? Who are they? (people)
> What is it? What are they? (places or things) (p. 40).

Example: Little Chuck Little, whose patience with all living things was phenomenal, said . . . (*To Kill a Mockingbird*, Lee, 1960, p. 28).

Teachers should find several examples from students' prior readings and help them find the appositives in each of the sentences provided. When you think the students recognize appositives, try this lesson plan (table 4.5).

The final rubric for the writing assignment should reflect students' mastery of all of the skills taught during this unit (see table 4.6).

Table 4.4. Lesson Plan

Lesson Title: The Answer to Wiesenthal's Question
Lesson Unit: *The Sunflower*

Lesson Purpose	As a result of today's lesson, students will be able to begin their summative writing assignment.
Essential Question	How does a moral person make moral decisions in an immoral world?
CCSS Standards	**W. 9–10.2:** Write informative texts to examine and convey complex ideas and concepts clearly and accurately though the effective selection, organization, and analysis of content.
	W. 9–10.2a: Introduce a topic; organize complex ideas, concepts and information to make important connections and distinctions.
	W. 9–10.2b: Develop the topic with well-chosen relevant and sufficient facts, extended definitions, concrete details, and quotations.
Academic CCSS Objectives for Instruction	**W. 9–10.2d:** Use precise language and domain-specific vocabulary to manage the complexity of the topic.
	W. 9–10.2f: Provide a concluding statement.
	L. 9–10.1b: Use various types of phrases to convey specific meanings and add variety and interest to writing.
	SL. 9–10.3: Evaluate a speaker's point of view, reasoning, and use of evidence and rhetoric, identifying any fallacious reasoning or exaggerated or distorted evidence.
	SL. 9–10.1: Initiate and participate effectively in a range of collaborative discussions with diverse partners, building on others' ideas and expressing their own clearly and persuasively.
	SL. 9–10.1d: Respond thoughtfully to diverse perspectives, summarize points of agreement and disagreement, and, when warranted, qualify or justify their own views and understandings and make new connections in light of the evidence and reasoning presented.

Habits of Mind Target	"Remaining open to continuous learning" (Costa & Kallick, 2009, p. x).
Student Outcome	As a result of participating in today's lesson, students will create their organizational strategy and write their thesis statements.
Warm up	1. Does your team's respondent agree with Wiesenthal? Why? Why not? 2. Do you agree with your team's respondent? Explain. 3. Do you think Wiesenthal made the right decision? Why? Why not? 4. Find out what each member of the team says about question 3 and be ready to report the answers to the class.
Guided Practice **LDC Template Tasks** Time	Essential Question: How does a moral person make moral decisions in an immoral world? After reading *The Sunflower*, write an essay that addresses the Essential Question of the text and support your position with evidence from the text, responses to his question, and your research. Be sure to include how the concepts of morality, forgiveness, atonement, and repentance affect your decision. Be sure to acknowledge opposing views, and to give examples from the text and your research that support your response to this question: Did Wiesenthal make the correct moral decision with the dying soldier? Step One: 1. Create an organizational strategy for this response. 2. Create a thesis statement. 3. Explain your position and provide support for your claims with evidence and warrants. 4. Explain the opposing position and provide counter-support for their claims with evidence and warrants. 5. Create a concluding statement that restates your position while showing respect for the opposing views.
Independent Practice Time	Step One: Decide on your position. Create a thesis statement for your essay. Find a peer editor on your team who will review and comment on your statement and rate it for clarity (does the reader know where you stand?), completeness (are there any missing essential elements?), and strength (thesis statement must be forceful, as it is the essential claim of the essay).
Assessment Time	Be ready to turn in your thesis statement and at least two sentences that will be included in the first paragraph of the essay. The opening paragraph includes the thesis statement and an indication of the organizational strategy being used for the essay.
Habits of Mind (10 points)	Create a rubric for evaluating students' participation skills during this phase. The rubric should measure attentiveness, thoughtfulness, appropriate questions, and quality of participation.
Closure Time	How do you know you're right?

Table 4.5. Lesson Plan

Lesson Title: Using Phrases and Clauses to Improve Writing
Lesson Unit: *The Sunflower*

Lesson Purpose	As a result of today's lesson, students will be able to improve their summative writing assignment.
Essential Question	How does a moral person make moral decisions in an immoral world?
CCSS Standards	**W. 9–10.2:** Write informative texts to examine and convey complex ideas and concepts clearly and accurately though the effective selection, organization, and analysis of content. **W. 9–10.2a:** Introduce a topic; organize complex ideas, concepts, and information to make important connections and distinctions. **W. 9–10.2b:** Develop the topic with well-chosen relevant and sufficient facts, extended definitions, concrete details and quotations.
Academic CCSS Objectives for Instruction	**W. 9–10.2d:** Use precise language and domain-specific vocabulary to manage the complexity of the topic. **W. 9–10.2f:** Provide a concluding statement. **L. 9–10.1b:** Use various types of phrases and clauses to convey specific meanings and add variety and interest to writing. **SL. 9–10.3:** Evaluate a speaker's point of view, reasoning, and use of evidence and rhetoric, identifying any fallacious reasoning or exaggerated or distorted evidence. **SL. 9–10.1:** Initiate and participate effectively in a range of collaborative discussions with diverse partners, building on others' ideas and expressing their own clearly and persuasively. **SL.9–10.1d:** Respond thoughtfully to diverse perspectives, summarize points of agreement and disagreement, and, when warranted, qualify or justify their own views and understandings and make new connections in light of the evidence and reasoning presented.
Habits of Mind Target	"Remaining open to continuous learning" (Costa and Kallick, 2009, p. x).
Student Outcome	As a result of participating in today's lesson, students will develop and/or refine their understanding of the use of appositives.
Warm up	1. What makes the following sentence interesting? "Gen Watanabe, the young man who worked as Mr. Hosokawa's translator, leaned over and spoke the words in Japanese to his employer" (Patchett, *Bel Canto*, as cited in Killgallon and Killgallon, 2007, p. 41). 2. Try the sentence without the words separated by commas; does it mean the same thing? 3. What do the words between the commas add to the sentence? 4. Change the words between the commas to different words and see if you can improve the sentence.

Guided Practice Time	Find four sentences that use appositives. Separate the appositives from the rest of the sentence and ask the students to do a matching exercise so they can determine which appositive belongs to the appropriate sentence. Example: Match 1. Judge Taylor was on the bench, his pilot fish writing rapidly below in front of him. — 1. and although he seemed to take his job casually 2. He was a man learned in the law, and that was the proof of the pudding. — 2. whose decisions were rarely overturned Next, write different words for each of the appositives in the sentences.
Independent Practice Time	After the students have completed the matching and rewriting exercises you have created for them, have each team provide its best sentence revision for the class to determine which team did the best job. A reward should be given to the team that was most successful.
Assessment Time	Add appositives to three sentences in your essay. Explain how and why each one is useful and adds to your writing style.
Closure Time	How does learning the writing craft help you with your writing skills?

Table 4.6. Performance Assessment Rubric

Score 4 Advanced	• The response demonstrates well-developed comprehension of the concepts of morality, forgiveness, repentance, and atonement. • The reasoning provided is logical, and ideas are well supported by evidence. • The connection between claims and evidence through the use of warrants is clear and logical. • The connections between Wiesenthal's response and the writer's points are relevant and meaningful. • The writing indicates that the student has gathered relevant information from multiple authoritative print and digital sources, using advanced searches effectively, and assessed the usefulness of each source in answering the research question. • The writing demonstrates that the information is integrated into the text selectively to maintain the flow of ideas, avoiding plagiarism and following a standard format for citation. • Phrases and clauses are well integrated into the writing.

(continued)

Table 4.6. *(Continued)*

Score 3 Proficient	• The response demonstrates a clear understanding of the concepts of morality, forgiveness, repentance, and atonement, but there is not the level of sophistication in thinking and writing that is found in the advanced response. • The reasoning provided is usually logical, and most ideas are supported by evidence. • The connections between Wiesenthal's response and the writer's points are usually relevant. • Warrants are used to connect claims and evidence. • There is a connection between the claim and justice. • The writing indicates that the student has gathered some relevant information from multiple authoritative print and digital sources, using advanced searches, and assessed the usefulness of most sources in answering the research question. • The writing demonstrates that the information is usually integrated into the text and the flow of ideas is apparent. The student has avoided plagiarism, and the writing follows a standard format for citation. • Most phrases and clauses add to the quality of the writing.
Score 2 Partially Proficient	• The response demonstrates some understanding of the concepts of morality, forgiveness, repentance, and atonement, but there is evidence that the writer does not have real mastery of these concepts. • The reasoning provided is logical at times, and some ideas are supported by evidence. • Warrants are not used consistently to connect claims and evidence. • There is a weak connection between Wiesenthal and this writing. • The writing indicates that the student has gathered a little relevant information from multiple print and digital sources, using advanced searches, and assessed the usefulness of some, but not all, sources in answering the research question. • The writing demonstrates that the information is not well integrated into the text, and the flow of ideas is not always apparent. The student has avoided plagiarism, and the writing follows a standard format for citation. • Some phrases and clauses are useful.
Score 1 Not Proficient	• The response demonstrates little or no understanding of the concepts of morality, forgiveness, repentance, and atonement. • The reasoning provided is illogical at times, and few ideas are supported by evidence. • Warrants are not used to connect claims and evidence. • There is no connection between Wiesenthal and this paper. • The writing indicates that the student has gathered very little if any relevant information from multiple print and digital sources. Instead of data, opinions are offered to support the claim. • The writing demonstrates that the information is not integrated into the text and the flow of ideas is not apparent. The student has not avoided plagiarism, and/or the writing does not include the standard format for citation. • There is no evidence that phrases and clauses have been mastered.

POINTS TO PONDER

This is a very intense unit. Both the reading and writing portions require maturity and thoughtfulness from the students. Discussions should be respectful, honest, and serious. Teachers may want to practice holding a discussion of that nature with a focus lesson plan before they expect their students to demonstrate those attributes. The deciding factor in all of this is the teacher. If teachers believe in their students' capacity to deal with sensitive, mature reading material and they believe in their own capacity to lead the students through this challenging unit, everyone will profit from this experience.

REFLECTIONS

At-risk students are closer to the realities of life than many of their peers. By yourself or with a partner, respond to the following:

1. *The Sunflower* provides an excellent example of good and evil, conflict and morality. How do these apply to twenty-first-century American adolescents?
2. "The Symposium" provides conflicting answers to a complex problem. How can at-risk students use this reading experience to help them in their own lives?
3. How will you help your students develop empathy as a result of reading this book?
4. How can this book help adolescents make sense of evil?
5. Why is it important to teach *The Sunflower*?

REFERENCES

Costa, A. L., & Kallick, B. (2009). *Habits of mind across the curriculum*. Alexandria, VA: ASCD.

www.chabad.org/library/article_cdo/aid/1010092/jewish/Should-We-Forgive-the-Nazis.

www.museumoftolearance.com.

Killgallon, D., & Killgallon, J. (2007). Grammar for high school: A sentence-composing approach. Portsmouth, NH: Heinemann.

Lee, H. (1960). *To kill a mockingbird*. New York: HarperCollins.

Wiesenthal, S. (1969). *The sunflower*. New York: Schocken Books.

5

HOW DOES A MORAL LEADER BRING HIS/HER VISION TO LIFE?

The only thing we have to fear is fear itself.

—President Franklin Delano Roosevelt

When World War II is studied in American schools, it is often taught in terms of the major battles, key players, questions surrounding America's entrance into the war, and so on. However, the speeches given during the war provide primary source material that can give students different insights into the conflicts, duplicity, and general confusion that were hallmarks of the war years.

Even leaders with good intentions and inspiring visions of a better tomorrow were capable of saying one thing and meaning another. For that reason, Franklin Delano Roosevelt's State of the Union Address, now known as the Four Freedoms Speech, will be examined to help students grapple with the historian's task of investigating, and help them understand history according to the upcoming Common Core.

IN THIS CHAPTER

In this chapter, the discussion will begin with examining the vocabulary in FDR's Four Freedoms Speech. Using predictions to teach vocabulary is a particularly useful strategy when working with at-risk students because it forces them to think critically about what words mean and how meaning is affected by context.

Following a vocabulary review, the rhetorical tools that FDR used so brilliantly will be studied. After the first of these reading-to-be-informed lessons has been reviewed, teachers will be shown a model for writing to inform where students will be asked to comment on contemporary challenges in light of President Roosevelt's visionary speech. In addition, a writing-to-persuade exercise will be provided for the students involved in this work at the end of the chapter.

FOUR FREEDOMS SPEECH: VOCABULARY

In the following lesson plan (table 5.1), students will be given the opportunity to review the key vocabulary terms and predict their meanings. Working in teams, students will be given a list of terms used in the speech. Teams will write down their predictions for what their terms mean. After all the teams' work has been completed, the class will determine if they agree with each team's predictions or not.

When the word is read in context, and carefully reviewed with the teacher, students will determine if they were able to predict wisely or not. Typically, struggling learners skip over words they do not understand or wait to be told what new words mean. Using this strategy helps all students become involved in vocabulary study.

Vocabulary Terms:

Unprecedented—Team 1
Enforced isolation—Team 2
Domination—Team 3
Tyranny—Team 4
Unilaterally—Team 5
Foreign peril—Team 1
Partisanship—Team 2
Antithesis—Team 3
Concentration camp—Team 4
Save—Team 5

Table 5.1. Lesson Plan

Lesson Title: Four Freedoms Speech
Lesson Unit: America during World War II

Lesson Overview	Provide a thorough understanding of America prior to its direct involvement in World War II. Essential Question: Is it ethical for an honest man to be duplicitous?
Academic Lesson Target Instructional	**Reading** **RI. Grades 11–12, Standard 4**: Determine the meaning of words and phrases as they are used in a text, including figurative, connotative, and technical meanings. **Writing** **SL. 11–12, Standard 3:** Evaluate a speaker's point of view. **Language**
Essential Question	How does a moral leader bring his/her vision to life?
Student Outcome	As a result of participating in this phase of the analysis of the speech, students will become aware of the use of critical terms as they provide insight into the author's stated and unstated agenda.
Habits of Mind Target	Listening with understanding and empathy.
Materials Needed	A copy of the Four Freedoms Speech for every student Placemat Vocabulary list
Warm up Time	List the four most important freedoms Americans enjoy. 1 2 3 4
Motivation Time	Suppose someone running for office suggests that equal freedom for American women should not be allowed. What would you do?
Guided Practice Time	After the teacher gives a brief overview of the speech, each team will be given its own list of terms. Each team will be given ten minutes to predict what each term means in the context of the speech. When the groups have completed their work, the class will determine whether or not the proposed definitions are likely to be correct.
Independent Practice Time	Teams will predict the meanings of the terms. The class will decide if the terms are correctly defined. The teacher will break the speech into sections and any vocabulary terms found in the sections will be correctly defined using this strategy. Students will keep track of how well they predicted the meanings of the terms.

(continue)

Table 5.1. *(Continued)*

Assessment Habit of Mind	Using informal observations, teachers determine how well each student has practiced and improved the targeted Habit of Mind skill, listening with understanding and empathy.
Assessment Content Time	Each student will compile a completed list of all the terms and indicate which terms were most important to the meaning of the speech.
Closure Time	Class returns to the Essential Question and reviews the students' progress at answering the question covered in the day's class.
Homework	BCR: How do writers use vocabulary effectively to promote the key ideas in their writing?

THE FOUR FREEDOMS SPEECH: RHETORIC

In 1940 France fell under the tyranny of the Nazi war machine. At that time, the Axis powers—Germany, the Fascists (in Italy), and Imperial Japan—had invaded and conquered significant portions of Europe and Asia. The only country in Western Europe not to fall under the invasion of the Nazis and Fascists was Great Britain. However, without cash and supplies, Roosevelt was warned by Churchill that Britain would not be able to withstand the Axis powers for very long. Although there were many Americans who believed in isolationism, Roosevelt was keenly aware that American involvement in World War II was just a matter of time.

Roosevelt had to walk a fine line between the politics of isolationism and the reality of re-elections. Therefore, during his third-term candidacy, he did not advocate involvement in the war. However, this speech was given after the election, when he could freely begin to outline his vision for a new world order which could only be accomplished by giving aid to our friends who were being attacked by our undeclared enemies. If one follows Roosevelt's logic in the Lend Lease Act, which he introduced in this speech, it seems reasonable to assume that a person lends the hose to a neighbor to put out the fire in his house only if the lender believes the danger to himself is imminent.

Roosevelt believed in the importance of this speech. "He started the now famous dictation session by calling to his secretary, 'Dorothy, take a law'" (Shulman, 2008, p. 105). The first two freedoms Roosevelt listed come directly from the Constitution. "The third globalized the programs of the New Deal, and a fourth . . . picked up on Woodrow Wilson's shattered vision for world peace" (Shulman, 2008, p. 105).

Using brilliant rhetorical devices, Roosevelt was able to share his visionary template for a stable and secure world after the war ended. There are those, however, who believe the speech was actually evil because they interpreted the speech to mean that government would take care of each individual and rob everyone of personal responsibility.

As students read the speech, they must be aware of the isolationists' perspectives, those who were fearful of big government, and the global chaos that the war created. Roosevelt had to describe a better future in the midst of a living nightmare. Therefore, any suggestion of a different future would be met with some level of cynicism and distrust from at least one faction.

Before This Lesson

Students should be taught a variety of rhetorical devices prior to the implementation of this lesson (table 5.2). They should understand the devices, their uses, and the effects the devices are expected to achieve before this lesson is taught. Teachers should list the essential rhetorical devices so that they are sure to be covered.

The challenge that Roosevelt faced when he gave this speech was to convince a reluctant and war-fearful American populace that no ocean was broad enough to secure America's borders. "Enduring peace cannot be bought at the cost of other people's freedom" (State of the Union Address, January 6, 1941).

Writing to Inform

The challenges facing Roosevelt in 1941 appeared to be the world at its worst. However, since the war ended, the Korean War, the conflict in Vietnam, and now the war against terrorism have shown us that being in a living nightmare does not end with the demise of one dictator or totalitarian form of government. The United States is surrounded by enemies from without and within as the domestic and international terrorist attacks in the United States will attest.

Table 5.2. Lesson Plan

Lesson Title: Four Freedoms Speech
Lesson Unit: America at War

Academic Lesson Target	As a result of today's lesson, students will be able to review the author's rhetoric in the Four Freedoms Speech to see how it advances the author's claims.
Essential Question	How does a moral leader bring his/her vision to life?
CCSS Strand	**RI. Grades 11–12, Strand 5:** Analyze and evaluate how the effectiveness of the structure an author uses in his or her exposition or argument, including whether the structure makes points clear, convincing, and engaging. **RI. Grades 11—12, Strand 6:** Determine an author's point of view or purpose in a text in which the rhetoric is particularly effective, analyzing how style and content contribute to the power, persuasiveness, or beauty of the text.
Student Outcome	Students will analyze FDR's use of rhetoric to advance his point of view in the Four Freedoms Speech.
Habits of Mind Target	Persistence
Materials Needed	Four Freedoms Speech for each student List of terms used for rhetorical analysis
Warm up Time	By yourself, and then with your team, respond to this quote: "At no previous time has American society been as seriously threatened from without as it is today." 1. What claim is the author making? 2. Which rhetorical device is being used? 3. Is it effective? 4. How do you know?
Motivation Time	There was no real winner after WWI and Americans did not want to fight in another foreign war. How do those feelings relate to how we feel about fighting in foreign wars today?
Guided Practice Time	Read the first two pages of the speech. 1. What rhetorical devices did FDR use? 2. Were they effective? 3. How do you know? We will go over all of these answers together.
Independent Practice Time	Read pp. 3–5. 1. What claims is FDR making? 2. What rhetorical devices did FDR use? 3. Were they effective? 4. How do you know? We will review some of the answers together.

Academic Assessment	By yourself, read p. 7. Alone, answer the following questions: 1. What claim is the author making? 2. What rhetorical devices did FDR use? 3. Were they effective? 4. How do you know?
Habits of Mind Assessment	Using informal assessments, evaluate each student's ability to listen with understanding and empathy.
Closure Time	How does the effective use of rhetoric advance an author's position?
Homework	Write a BCR. Be sure to include at least three rhetorical devices. We need one more freedom today. It is X because ____________.

During one week in April of 2013, North Korea threatened to send up a test nuclear missile; the Boston Marathon was the scene of domestic terrorism; and Iran's nuclear threat grew stronger. Recently Great Britain has called on help from the United States to avoid acts of terrorism; South Korea expects us to protect its borders; and Israel is very vulnerable to any attack from its Arab neighbors, especially those who have nuclear capabilities.

It should be reasonably simple for students to compare and contrast the worlds of 1941 and 2013 on the premise that "We must help our neighbors if we hope to protect ourselves." At-risk students are very sensitive to issues concerning loyalty and support to friends. This lesson (table 5.3) should resonate with them.

How This Speech Evolved

Most at-risk students are reluctant writers and feel even less inclined to revise and edit their work. For this reason, a monograph written by Laura Crowell (1955) has special utility here. In this study, the seven drafts of the Four Freedoms Speech are carefully reviewed to demonstrate how careful editing led to the creation of a powerful speech. Although Roosevelt dictated the first five pages rather spontaneously, "its seven drafts offer the rhetorical critic excellent opportunity for studying the step-by-step development of a significant address" (Crowell, 1955, p. 266).

Table 5.3. Lesson Plan

Lesson Title: Writing to Inform—Comparison/Contrast Essay
Lesson Unit: America at War

Lesson Overview	Write an informative essay. Essential Question: Is the United States similar to or different from the United States in 1941?
Academic Lesson Target Instructional **Essential Question**	**Reading** **Writing** **RW. 2, Grades 11–12:** Write informative essay to examine and convey complex ideas, concepts, and information clearly through the effective selection, organization, and analysis of content. **Speaking and Listening** **Language** How does a moral leader bring his/her vision to life?
Student Outcome	Each student will develop an informative essay that clearly delineates the similarities and differences in the United States today and in 1941 along the construct of our need to support our allies.
Habits of Mind Target	Persistence
Materials Needed	Access to Google Scholar and other internet sites Venn diagram
Warm up Time	Which countries are our friends? List two. Which countries are our enemies? List two.
Motivation Time	What do we need from our friends (allies)? What do they need from us? What can happen if we don't help each other?
Guided Practice Time	Using a Venn diagram, compare and contrast the worlds of 1941 and 2013 according to our support for our allies.
Independent Practice Time	Create an outline that shows the skeleton of the essay. When the teacher has approved of the outline, each student will begin to write his/her rough draft.
Assessment Habit of Mind Time	Rough drafts are due for peer editing the next class session. Using informal observations, teachers determine how well each student has practiced and improved the targeted Habit of Mind skill.
Closure Time	Class returns to the Essential Question.
Homework	Students write their rough drafts.

After the president's original five-page draft was created, according to Crowell (1955), Benjamin Cohen, Harry Hopkins, Robert Sherwood, and Sam Rosenman helped him with the development of each draft. Students often believe that reflection and revision are unnecessary components of effective writing; however, as this monograph clearly shows, it was the careful crafting of each major facet of the speech that gave the speech its rhetorical brilliance.

For example, in the first draft of the speech, Roosevelt wrote: "America has not in the past faced the threat of domination; the present problem is unique" (Crowell, 1955, p. 268). After several drafts, each of which tried to compress the idea into a pithy phrase, the seventh and final draft reads as follows: "There is unity in the United States today" (Crowell, 1955, p. 268).

One important facet of the speech which Roosevelt wanted to emphasize is the uniqueness of the time; he ended the speech by forcibly restating this theme: the country is facing an unprecedented situation. Since he could not declare war explicitly, he could underscore the imminent and terrible danger facing America at the time of the speech.

Another example of how the careful revisions led to greater clarity is the original "in the guidance of God under liberty" to "in freedom under the guidance of God" (Crowell, 1955, p. 273). This change in emphasis resonates with the American people who believe that "under God people rule" (Crowell, 1955, p. 273).

Roosevelt used the term "Australasia" to identify Australia and all the lands in the southwest section of the Pacific Ocean. From here, he was able to create the metaphor which captures the reality that the South Pacific was facing. In an earlier draft, this was expressed as "any attempt to lock it into an attic room while the procession of civilization goes past the door" (Crowell, 1955, p. 274). However, in the final draft he changes a hypothetical attic to the real events in the world. The final draft reads "any attempt to lock us behind an ancient Chinese wall while the procession of civilization went past" (Crowell, 1955, p. 274).

In order to help struggling learners understand that effective rhetoric comes from multiple revisions and thoughtful consideration of how to match purpose to purposeful language, it is important to give them the opportunity to look at some of the revisions and analyze how the changes made the speech stronger (see table 5.4).

Table 5.4. Lesson Plan

Lesson Title: Rhetoric
Lesson Unit: America at War

Academic Lesson Target	As a result of today's lesson, students will be able to read the Four Freedoms Speech as it evolved in order to understand how revision and reflection are critical to effective rhetoric.
Essential Question	How does a moral leader bring his/her vision to life?
CCSS Strand	**RI. Grades 11-12. Strand 6:** Determine an author's point of view in a text in which the rhetoric is particularly effective, analyzing how style and content contribute to the power and persuasiveness of the text.
Student Outcome	Students will be able to read and analyze several drafts and determine how the revisions added to the effectiveness of the rhetoric used.
Habits of Mind Target	Persistence
Materials Needed	Lesson Plan Four Freedoms Speech
Warm up Time	Revise these statements so they are clearer: The ball was hit by the boy. People need to know what to do in an emergency so they can keep safe. Persistence, ability to wait, and perseverance lead to success.
Motivation Time	What is the purpose of editing your own writing? What are some of the possible benefits of careful editing?
Guided Practice Time	In one early draft, Roosevelt wrote "I hope that none of us will be beguiled," but the final draft read as follows: "In fulfillment of this purpose we will not be intimidated." What are the fundamental differences between the two drafts? How does the new rhetoric clarify the ideas?
Independent Practice Time	With your team, answer the above questions for the following: 1. "People in charge of production" becomes "The men in charge of the program." 2. "Faith in the guidance of God under liberty" becomes "faith in freedom under the guidance of God." 3. "Yesterday's best is not good enough for today" becomes "Today's best is not good enough for tomorrow."
Assessment Time	By yourself: "Congress must be kept informed" to "Congress must rightly keep itself informed."
Closure Time	Why is it important for a writer to revise, reflect, and rewrite in order to achieve a successful and effective speech?
Homework	Revise your latest BCR to make your points more clear and emphatic.

The following is a template that can be used to help peer editors review the paper that another student has written:

Score 4

The paper supports its claims with evidence and credible warrants filled with supporting information.	Yes___	No___
The paper shows that it has been revised for basic writing skills.	Yes___	No___
The writer used rhetorical devices to support strong points in the writing.	Yes___	No___
The writing is clear, logical, and filled with rhetorical devices used effectively.	Yes___	No___

Score 3

The paper supports almost all of its claims with evidence and credible warrants.	Yes___	No___
The paper shows that most of the basic writing problems have been revised.	Yes___	No___
The writer used rhetorical devices.	Yes___	No___
The writing is clear enough that it is possible to follow the writer's logic.	Yes___	No___

Score 2

The paper only provides evidence and warrants for some claims.	Yes___	No___
The paper still contains many writing problems.	Yes___	No___
The writer did not use rhetorical devices.	Yes___	No___
The writing is illogical, and there is no connection made between the important points in the writing.	Yes___	No___

Writing to Persuade

Although he failed to attribute his source, Roosevelt was really paraphrasing Benjamin Franklin, who said, "They that give up liberty to obtain a little temporary safety deserve neither liberty nor safety." One of the reasons this saying has lasted is because it brings on such conflicting feelings. Especially after 9/11, Americans seemed more willing to give up privacy rights rather than to risk another attack. Twelve years later, the mood of the country has shifted slightly, but the recent attack at the Boston Marathon brought back memories of our vulnerability and Franklin's thoughts are even more prominent now than before.

During this writing-to-persuade activity (table 5.5), students will be asked to take a stand on this topic. Should we be willing to lose some of our privacy and other liberties in order to protect ourselves or will losing our liberties protect neither our safety nor our freedoms?

POINTS TO PONDER

Roosevelt gave his speech during a very turbulent point in history. Since then every American president has been faced with conflicting and potentially dangerous situations that have required courage, vision, and humility. Since the threat of nuclear war seems to be a permanent part of the landscape, our students need to be able to recognize true visionary thinking when they hear it, rather than blindly accept the expedient and easy answer.

In this chapter, students are faced with the challenge of reading a piece of informative text that helped to shape America's foreign policy from that time until now. The text requires sensitivity to rhetorical devices in order to appreciate the writer's stated and unstated agendas.

Students have been given the opportunity to study vocabulary and rhetoric, and to practice writing to inform and persuade during their work on this speech. At-risk students may not embrace these exercises unless they can see the points made from their own perspectives. They, too, have to make difficult decisions that affect other's lives. This work gives them practice at using higher-order thinking skills in their own life experiences.

REFLECTIONS

This chapter requires thoughtful work on problem-solving skills, vocabulary acquisition, and recognizing and using persuasive language. By yourself or with a partner reflect on the following:

1. Roosevelt knew that he was going to enter the war, but even after the election he did not announce his plans during his State of the Union Address. Some believe that he was less than honest in this speech. How will you reconcile this and the description of Roosevelt's being a moral leader with your students?

Table 5.5. Lesson Plan

Lesson Title: Writing to Persuade
Lesson Unit: America at War

Lesson Overview	Each student will write a persuasive essay. Essential Question: Is it wiser to protect our liberty or lose some liberty to protect our safety?
Academic Lesson Target Instructional **Essential Question**	**Reading** **Writing** **RW. 1 Grades 11–12, Strand 1:** Write arguments to support claims in an analysis of liberty versus safety and use valid reasoning and relevant and sufficient evidence. **Speaking and Listening** **Language** How does a moral leader bring his/her vision to life?
Student Outcome	Students will write a persuasive essay defending or arguing against the curtailment of certain freedoms in order to protect the population from terrorism.
Habits of Mind Target	Persistence
Materials Needed	Access to Google Scholar or other websites that have pertinent information
Warm up Time	List four freedoms you have as American citizens. Put a check next to the ones you would not be willing to lose.
Motivation Time	Would you want an armed police officer walking the halls of this school in order to protect us?
Guided Practice Time	In light of the Newtown School shooting, the Boston Marathon, and other terrorist attacks, are there fundamental freedoms you are willing to lose? If so, organize your essay arguing against Franklin's comment. If you think that losing freedom is never warranted, organize your essay in support of Franklin. In any case, use specific information to support your claims.
Independent Practice Time	Create an outline that shows the skeleton of the essay. When the teacher has approved of the outline, each student will begin to write his/her rough draft.
Assessment Time **Habit of Mind**	Rough drafts are due for peer editing the next class session. Using informal observations, teachers determine how well each student has practiced and improved at being persistent.
Closure Time	Class returns to the Essential Question.
Homework	Students write their rough drafts for the next class.

2. Roosevelt used rhetorical devices in this speech. How will you convince your at-risk students that knowing and using rhetoric is important to them?
3. Would you start the conversation about students being willing to lose liberties to protect security by discussing the idea of armed guards in schools? Explain.
4. How can you help your struggling learners develop their problem-solving skills by teaching the Four Freedoms Speech?
5. How can you use peer editing to improve your students' writing skills?

REFERENCES

Crowell, L. (1955). The building of the "four freedoms" speech, *Speech Monographs, 22*(5), 266–283.

Shulman, M. R. (2008). The four freedoms: Good neighbors make good law and good policy in a time of insecurity. *Fordham Law Review, 77* (November): 2.

State of the Union Address (1941). www.amiericanrhetoric.com/speeches/fdrthe fourfreedoms.htm.

6

AT-RISK STUDENTS AND MATHEMATICS AND THE COMMON CORE

> As far as laws of math refer to reality, they are certain, and as far as they are certain, they do not refer to reality.
>
> —Albert Einstein

For more than a decade, researchers looking at high school mathematics in high-performing countries have determined that the American high school mathematics curriculum is flawed and must become seriously more focused and coherent in order to accomplish significant changes in achievement in mathematics in this country. According to corestandards.org, "The current standards are a mile wide and an inch deep" (www.corestandards.org/Math, p. 1). It is hoped that the new CCSS in mathematics will provide a focused response to the current problem.

The Common Core Standards in math clearly state what students should understand and be able to do. The standards stress conceptual understanding, but also constantly return to such organizing principles as place value or the laws of arithmetic to structure these ideas (www.corestandards.org/Math).

Ultimately, teachers must determine what evidence they will accept that the student has achieved mastery of the mathematical principles he/she has used. Depending on the student's maturity, he/she should be able to justify

> why a particular mathematical statement is true or where a mathematical rule comes from. There is a world of difference between a student who can summon a mnemonic device to expand a product . . . and a student who can explain where the mnemonic comes from.
>
> The student who can explain the rule understands the mathematics. . . . Mathematical understanding and procedural skills are equally important, and both are assessable using mathematical tasks of sufficient richness. (http://corestandards.org/Math, p. 2)

If all students came to school with the prior knowledge and understanding taught in the previous grade, and no students suffered from math anxiety, it would be easy to initiate the standards in all classrooms. However, that is clearly not the case.

IN THIS CHAPTER

In too many school classrooms, there is a wide variety of feelings of antipathy regarding math, varying levels of prior knowledge in math, and a wide scope of student resistance to attempting to learn any new mathematical skills. In this chapter, to cover these issues, a brief overview of the upcoming Common Core Standards in Mathematics will be provided. Next, the causes, effects, and some possible cures for math anxiety will be discussed. Finally, issues specifically related to what at-risk students need in order to succeed in mathematics will be examined.

OVERVIEW OF COMMON CORE STANDARDS IN MATHEMATICS

According to key players who worked on the Common Core Standards in Mathematics, students will be expected "to practice applying mathematical ways of thinking to real-world issues and challenges; students are expected to think and reason mathematically across the major strands and to understand the connections found among such mathematical arenas as geometry, algebra, probability, and statistics" (Porton, 2013b, p. 94).

"One hallmark of mathematical understanding is the ability to justify, in a way appropriate to the student's mathematical maturity, *why* a particular mathematical statement is true or where a mathematical rule comes from" (Common Core State Standards Initiative). As a result, students need to be taught not only what to do, and in what order, but the *how* and the *why*.

According to http://corestandards.org/Math, the states that have adopted the Common Core State Standards will follow a coherent scope and sequence to be sure that all students can do the following:

1. Make sense of problems and persevere in solving them.
2. Reason abstractly and quantitatively.
3. Construct viable arguments and critique the reasoning of others.
4. Model with mathematics.
5. Use appropriate tools.
6. Attend to precision.
7. Look for and make use of structure.
8. Look for and express regularity in reasoning.

In addition, according to www.corestandards.org/assets/CCSSI_Mathematics_Appendix_A.pdf, for students who are in need of additional support, using strategies consistent with Response to Intervention practices can be helpful. In a school that develops a school-wide community of support for all students, struggling learners will find more success.

Providing students in need of additional instruction with another math support class during the school day can build students' self-confidence. Where after-school tutoring is available, students with a strong locus of control can avail themselves of extra help. Finally, extended time during the summer to help struggling math learners maintain or develop their math proficiency can help more students succeed.

Research in this field suggests that the goal of the standards "should be to provide support so that all students can reach the college and career ready line by the end of the eleventh grade" (www.corestandards.org/assets/CCSSI_Mathematics_Appendix_A.pdf, p. 5). In the next section, how math anxiety can compromise even potentially talented math students will be discussed.

MATH ANXIETY

Math anxiety is defined as "a feeling of tension, apprehension or fear that interferes with math" (Ashcraft, 2002, p. 181). Alternatively, it is defined as an "irrational dread of mathematics that interferes with manipulation of numbers and solving mathematical problems within a variety of everyday life and academic situations" (as cited in Furner & Berman, 2003, p. 170). The effects of this disorder are fairly consistent over time. Normally intelligent individuals who perform everyday tasks without difficulty find themselves immobilized in the face of a mathematical task, course, or assignment.

There are many causes for this problem. The issues involved with poor teaching will be discussed later; however, it is important to note that some teaching styles, texts, and teachers' prior training have been implicated as possible risk factors.

Cultural factors, such as the widespread acceptance that math is really a male domain, are exemplified in the Barbie doll that used to say, "Math is hard." It seems that there are many cultural and social forces that work against women's success in math. Stereotypical thinking by family, peers, and teachers only reinforces negative gender bias against females' success in mathematics.

People who suffer from math anxiety take fewer elective math courses and/or elect to take the most fundamental math courses instead of attempting to take more advanced math classes. When they take any math classes, they typically receive lower grades. This may be the result of their reluctance to take chances or try alternative approaches, or their own negative schema about the value of math in their lives.

This is not just a matter of "self-perception." As cited in Furner and Berman (2003), in 1989, the National Council of Teachers of Mathematics (NCTM) recognized math anxiety as a substantial difficulty and established criteria to help assess students' mathematical dispositions. NCTM suggests that teachers assess students'

- confidence in using math to solve problems, communicate ideas, and reason;
- flexibility in exploring mathematical ideas and trying a variety of methods when solving problems;
- willingness to persevere in mathematical tasks;
- interests, curiosity, and inventiveness in doing math;
- ability to reflect on and monitor their own thinking and performance while doing math;
- focus on value of and appreciation for math in relation to its real-life application, connections to other disciplines, existence in other cultures, use as a tool for learning, and characteristics as a language (p. 233).

One of the most disastrous results of math anxiety is that most American high school graduates leave high school far below minimum standards for mathematical proficiency and literacy (Furner & Berman, 2003). The CCSS is designed to change these results and ensure that every student has access to rigorous mathematical instruction.

Causes

There are numerous causes for math anxiety. One of the earliest influences comes from the home, where parents share their negative perceptions regarding math, its usefulness, or their belief that their children will not be able to succeed in math because they did not succeed.

When children enter school and start kindergarten, they enter the world of elementary school teachers. Many early childhood educators have their own issues with math and those feelings are shared, modeled, and reinforced with their students. A negative schema regarding math is easily reinforced if a child experiences problems with math and is surrounded by adults who suffer from their own math anxiety.

Differentiation is required during math instruction as students who use different learning styles and have varying academic skills and interests need different scaffolding. One size does not fit all in any instruction, but it is especially true in math precisely because of math anxiety.

However, there are specific behaviors that some misguided teachers use when teaching math that create a negative and unsafe climate during math instruction. For example, requiring one correct way to solve a problem diminishes experimentation with other ways of looking at a math question. It inhibits reflection on various possibilities for solving problems and leaves discouragement where there could have been curiosity.

Finally, assigning math problems as a way of punishing students could not be more effective at reinforcing students' negative feelings toward math. Teachers who engage in such behavior can expect to see lower test scores, negative attitudes, and resistance to tackling math problems from their students.

Teachers, however, cannot be held accountable for all of the students who display math anxiety. They cannot always prevent math anxiety, but they can help to reduce it. In order to reduce math anxiety, teachers can use writing assignments to help students think mathematically in writing. Challenging students to think critically and creatively can help even the most reluctant math student to take risks in understanding and enjoying math.

Marzano's Dimensions of Learning (1992), specifically Dimension One, emphasizes the importance of a safe learning environment where students are encouraged to take chances and are awarded for their effort as well as their performance. If students are to overcome their math anxiety, they must believe they can perform mathematical operations as well as their peers. In an emotionally safe learning environment, errors are considered a natural part of the learning process. Reluctant math students can find success in just such a learning climate.

Finally, the NCTM (1989) offers some sound suggestions for reducing math anxiety that have not been covered yet in this section. They suggest creating a variety of testing environments, refraining from tying self-esteem to success in math, and emphasizing that everyone makes mistakes in math.

Placing encouraging quotes in the classroom and displaying successful work from students who don't usually succeed creates a warm, positive climate. Allowing for cooperative learning can help students use "kidspeak" to explain difficult concepts to each other. Emphasizing the importance of creative, high-quality thinking over rote manipulation of formulas is an important step to helping students understand that math is a human endeavor that is filled with learning through trial and error.

Bad Teaching and Math Anxiety

In elementary schools, teachers are certified if they have majored in primary or elementary school education and met the certification requirements for their home state. In middle schools, where there is no current middle school certification process, "Just one-third of middle school math teachers have a degree in mathematics or math education" (Robelen, 2013, p. 1). Fewer than half of the elementary school teachers surveyed feel they are well prepared to teach math or science (Robelen, 2013).

Due to various issues, many teachers fail to place a high priority on asking students to explain or justify their work, being satisfied with correct products rather than actual understanding of the process. This runs counter to the goals of CCSS in mathematics and leaves many students unprepared to meet the new challenges.

The CCSS in mathematics promotes the importance of reasoning and making sense of mathematical principles. However, many teachers begin their lessons by explaining a concept and then assigning an activity to reinforce and practice it. Students facing CCSS in mathematics will be unprepared for the new challenges if they have only been instructed in the unprofitable memorize, practice, and repeat methodology.

Even if the teacher has solid training, has a positive attitude toward trial and error in math instruction, and encourages inquiry, if the textbook in use is dull, misguided, or can be considered an inconsiderate text, students will suffer. At the present time, there are few textbooks available that match the emphasis and pedagogy of the CCSS in math. However, once the assessments have been made available, it is reasonable to assume that the newest textbooks will match the current trends in mathematical education.

WHAT DO STRUGGLING LEARNERS NEED IN ORDER TO SUCCEED IN MATH?

In this section, some of the root causes of at-risk behaviors will be examined. Next, the connection between the at-risk behaviors and math anxiety will be made. Finally, some suggestions for helping struggling learners to develop a more positive schema will be provided.

In order to understand at-risk learners, it is important to review some of their deeply held beliefs. For example, taken from a student's point of view, Sagor's (1993) "characteristics of the discouraged learner" would be as follows:

> The world is a place over which I have little or no control. Things just happen, and there isn't much I can do to change most situations. When things in life become difficult, my best defense is to avoid the situation. Most adults are not to be trusted. They may act like they care about you, but they really don't. My future is not very exciting. I will have very little money but very many problems. There is not much I can do to change my future. School is usually very boring. Teachers do not tell us why we have to do most of their work, and they get angry when I ask them why we are doing a long, boring assignment. When I really get bored, I get into trouble just to keep myself awake. I learn better if I can see the practical application of what is being taught. Effort has very little to do with success. (Porton, 2013a, p. 20)

On a Personal Note

I was intrigued by the literature on at-risk students and created a writing assignment for my struggling learners to see how closely theory and reality were aligned. Below is an actual response from one of my students:

Dear Mrs. Porton,

I feel that the world is a place over which I have no control. Things do just happen and there isn't much I can do to change most situations. I've never been able to handle things on my own. I feel like there is no way to coupe [cope] with a problem or tragedy without help. Except me, I can't get help with my situations. I know because my problems haven't been solved, they just got worse.

I do usually avoid my problems by blocking them out. If I don't hear them or don't know them then theirs not a problem. The best answer is to avoid a situation because it's never gonna change. I know because I've been there.

I will never trust adults again. All the adults including my parents, that I trusted lied, cheated or said the wrong thing. They do act like they care and want to help but they stab you right in the back. How do I know? Because my parents and ex friends did the same thing.

I can't talk about stuff better then writing about it. It's easier to write it down and keep it to yourself then to talk about it and have someone tell someone else. I guess you would call it trust, and that's something I couldn't or won't give anyone. My trust in them. I can't.

You never know what will happen next. The future is just like a surprise. People who do good one day, their just lucky. But it makes me mad to see someone brag. Especially since I'm below average. It's not helpful though when your family and friends call you worthless. (Porton, 2013a, p. 21)

Connections between At-risk Learners and Math Anxiety

In order to understand the correlations between at-risk students and math anxiety, it is important to begin the discussion with issues surrounding attribution and locus of control. "Attributions are the explanations that people give as to why they were successful or not" (Porton, 2013a, p. 28).

According to many attributer theorists, there are three sets of characteristics normally associated with attributions. First, people believe that their success, or failure, is due to effort or luck. The former indicates someone who has an internal locus of control, the latter represents someone who has an external locus of control. People believe the causes of their victories or failures are stable over time, or are unpredictable and subject to change. For example, a student who believes that hard work leads to success works hard all the time. However, a student who believes that success is the result of luck or ease of the task sees no reason for consistent effort.

Does the person believe he/she can control the cause of success? If so, effort will be made by the individual to manage all the variables possible to safeguard success. However, if the causes of success or failure are beyond control, there is no reason to try to influence the outcome.

Students who have an internal locus of control modify their behavior in order to influence the outcome. If the work habits result in achievements, there is no reason to change what is being done. However, if the work habits are not meeting with success, the student will change the habits that are being counterproductive.

Lynch, Hurford, and Cole (2002) believe that students who have an internal locus of control experience more success in school. They are academic risk-takers; they accept feedback; they persist; they know they can succeed. The opposite is true of students who have an external locus of control.

Unfortunately, the vast number of struggling learners fall under the category of external locus of control. As Sagor (1993) points out, it is important to remember that their parents often mirror the same dynamics. Convincing multiple generations that effort can lead to success is a daunting but important task. If a person does not believe he/she had anything to do with either success or failure, there is no pride in success and no ownership of failure (Porton, 2013a).

When we examine math-anxiety-laden behavior against the results of an external locus of control, the overlap is impressive. Students who do not believe they can control what happens to them do very little work, take few chances, and rarely persist when faced with challenging tasks.

As a result, attributional issues are reinforced by repeated failure. "Math is too hard, so why should I try since I can't do it anyway?" becomes the mantra of the reluctant learner. This belief system frequently leads to an unexamined life. One of the features of those with math anxiety is that they do not reflect on their thinking and performance. The reasoning goes "This is all out of my control. What is there to think about?"

SUITABLE STRATEGIES FOR SUCCESS

The following list, given in no particular order, is designed to promote creative thinking for reaching and teaching mathematics to struggling learners.

1. Display a sample problem and have the class, working in teams, determine what they think they know about the problem, what they need to learn, and which possible mathematical principles could apply.
2. Create a graphic organizer based on the results of the students' predictions.
3. Display some of the key terms pertinent to the new problem and ask students to predict their meanings.

4. Ask students to volunteer their ideas to the question, "What would happen if I try X?"
5. "Use the five-step problem-solving model:
   a. Restate the problem
   b. Find needed data
   c. Plan what to do
   d. Find the solution. Step 1 Step 2 Step 3
   e. Check your work for errors" (Barton & Heidema, 2002, p. 100).
6. Create concept circles for categorizing words and terms (Vacca & Vacca, 2002) (see figure 6.1).
   a. Choose terms with common attributes or relationships;
   b. Put the selected terms in the four sections of the circle;
   c. Tell students to identify the common attributes or discover the relationships among the terms.
7. 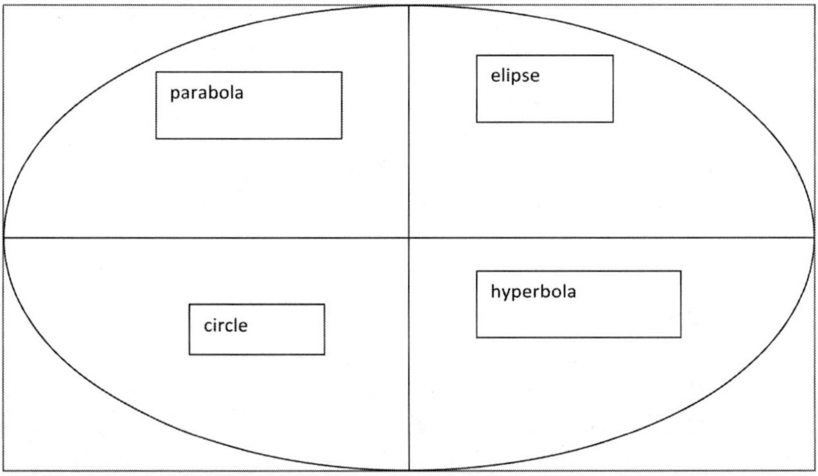

Figure 6.1.

8. Use a Venn diagram to contrast and compare concepts.
9. Use humor in the stories that you create that require students to solve problems.

POINTS TO PONDER

The goal of this chapter has been to review what teachers of mathematics need to know about struggling learners and math anxiety. The goal was not to introduce mathematical principles, skills, or knowledge regarding math. The assumption has been that math teachers know math; they run into difficulty when they try to teach what they know to students who don't want, or are unwilling to try, to learn math.

Math anxiety is a recognized disorder which compromises cognitively healthy individuals and prevents them from attempting any math, whether in an academic or real-world situation. Suggestions were provided for making the connection and closing the gap between mathematics instruction and at-risk learners.

REFLECTIONS

The goal of this chapter is to help math teachers understand the mind-set of at-risk learners in math. By yourself or with a partner, reflect on the following:

1. How does an external locus of control affect a student's willingness to try a difficult subject?
2. How can using humor in math examples affect the climate in a math class?
3. How can teachers help move students from an external locus of control to a more internal locus of control?
4. Why do math teachers need to understand the mind-set of their struggling learners?
5. What will you do differently as a result of reading this chapter?

REFERENCES

Ashcraft, M. H. (2002). Math anxiety: Personal, educational, and cognitive consequences. *Current Directions in Psychological Science, 11*(5) (October 2002): 181.

Barton, M. L., & Heidema. (2002). *Teaching reading in mathematics* (2nd ed.). Aurora, CO: Mid-continental Research for Education and Learning.

Common Core State Standards Initiative (2012). www.corestandards.org.

Furner, J. M., & Berman, B. T. (2003). Review of research: Math anxiety: Overcoming a major obstacle to the improvement of student math performance. *Childhood Education, 79*(3), 170–174.

Hilton, P. (2013). *The Two-Year College Mathematics Journal, 11*(3), 174–188.

Lynch, S., Hurford, D. P., & Cole, A. (2002). Parental enabling attitudes and locus of control of at-risk and honors students. *Adolescence, 37*(147), 527–549.

Marzano, R. J. (1992). *A different kind of classroom: Teaching with dimensions of learning*. Alexandria, VA: Association for Supervision and Curriculum Development.

National Council of Teachers of Mathematics (1989). Curriculum and evaluation standards for school mathematics. Reston, VA: Author.

Porton, H. D. (2013a). *Helping struggling learners succeed in school.* Boston: Pearson.

Porton, H. D. (2013b) *Teaching the standards: How to blend common core state standards into secondary instruction.* Lanham, MD: Rowman & Littlefield.

Rebora, A. (2013). Math teachers strive to bring core to at-risk students. Retrieved from www.edweek.org/tm/articles/2013/03/13/ccio_math_at-risk.html?tkn=ZPZFo3x3X5.

Robelen, E. W. (2013). Common Science Standards face capacity issues. *Education Week, 15* (31), 1–12.

Sagor, R. (1993). *At-risk students: Reaching and teaching them.* Swampscott, MA: Watersun Publishing.

Vacca, R. T., & Vacca, A. L. (2002). Writing across the curriculum. In R. Indrisano & James R. Squire (Eds.), *Perspectives in writing: Research, theory, and practice,* 214–250. Washington, DC: International Reading Association.

7

DISCOURAGED LEARNERS AND COMMON CORE STATE STANDARDS IN SCIENCE

The important thing is not to stop questioning.

—Albert Einstein

The Next Generation Science Standards (NGSS), developed by a coalition of twenty-six states and several national organizations, are complete and almost ready for adoption by individual states. Once the Next Generation Science Standards are adopted, the biggest task will be to bring the standards to life in classrooms across the country.

The NGSS match the Common Core in that they both seek greater depth of understanding science and ask students to be able to apply their new knowledge through inquiry and engineering design. "The science and engineering practices embedded in the new science standards have considerable synergy with the practices and skills promoted in the common core math and literary standards" (Robelen, 2013a, p. 12).

Unlike the English/language arts and math standards, organizations involved with the new science standards are urging a "go slow" approach. Experts believe that obstacles such as high costs, professional development, and adequate assessment instruments require a slow-but-steady approach to implementation.

It is imperative that organizations that helped to develop the new standards, such as Achieve, remain a part of developing the assessments to be sure that there is alignment among goals, strategies, and assessments. Currently, that vision is being realized.

IN THIS CHAPTER

In this chapter, an overview of the new standards will be provided and challenges that currently face the implementation of CCSS in science will be discussed. Next, Robert Marzano (2013) has created a paradigm for looking at levels of questions that will have enormous utility for curriculum writers and classroom teachers working in science. Finally, a brief discussion of writing in science will be provided.

OVERVIEW OF CCSS IN SCIENCE

At the present time, there is no specific date given for the implementation of the CCSS in science. Now that the Next Generation Science Standards (NGSS) have been completed, the next steps involve piloting the new standards and putting them forward for adoption by the states.

The NGSS are expected to spell out in much greater detail the specifics involved for each science course. It is expected that by the time the CCSS in science are ready for implementation, the NGSS will have articulated the science-specific standards that each discipline in science will be expected to use to teach content in compliance with the CCSS standards for literacy in the sciences (Porton, 2013).

At the center of the standards in science are "performance expectations that ask students to take actions to show their learning, such as plan and conduct investigations, analyze and interpret data, and devise models" (Robelen, 2013a). This is a quantum leap from completing worksheets, note-taking, and memorizing.

"According to the reading standards for literacy in science, in grades nine and ten, students should be able to cite specific textual evidence to support analysis of science texts" (Porton, 2013, p. 130). Students must deal with precise details of explanations and descriptions. Science requires attention to detail in order to keep readers alert to essential information. All students must have access to grade-level complex texts. "Complex text is a rich repository of ideas, information, and experience which all readers should learn how to access, although some students will need more scaffolding to do so" (Coleman & Pimentel, 2012, p. 3).

At-risk students may need extra help with fluency practice and vocabulary development. Even if students require extra scaffolding, they should not miss out on important practice and instruction that will help them to read closely, think deeply, participate actively, and gain knowledge with their peers.

"Students are also expected to recognize central ideas or conclusions of a text and be able to trace the explanation or depiction of complex processes. They must also follow with precision a complex, multistep procedure when carrying out experiments. Teachers must also provide the scaffolding needed to help students attend to special cases or exceptions" (Porton, 2013, p. 130).

Students must also be able to analyze the structure of relationships among key concepts in a text and see the relationships between key terms. Only in science and math are students required to be able to translate quantitative or technical information from words to charts and graphs and back again.

It should be clear that all these tasks pose serious challenges for discouraged learners. They are not typically strong readers and the rigorous and complex language typical of science texts makes most texts unfriendly and unapproachable. It is up to the teacher to provide the necessary scaffolding to help all students reach the goals of CCSS in science, that is, develop "these larger cognitive structures by identifying knowledge and skills, organizing these elements sequentially and progressively, and then infusing more cognitive complexity into the knowledge-acquisition process" (Common Core State Standards Initiative, 2012, p. 2).

At-risk learners need scaffolding in order to be able to comprehend complex ideas and evaluate evidence found in content-rich texts. "Scaffolds enable all students to experience rather than avoid the complexity of the text. Many students will need careful instruction—including effective scaffolding—to enable them to read at the level of text complexity required by the Common Core State Standards" (Coleman & Pimentel, 2012, p. 8).

At-risk learners need to begin everything in concrete terms; they need to see all the evidence arrayed and organized before they can proceed. As they grow, they will learn how to use their prior knowledge to test their hypotheses during the scientific process. Teachers need to provide the scaffolding with the vocabulary that will be encountered, offer many opportunities to use content knowledge, and propose increasingly challenging problems as students' expertise develops.

CHALLENGES FACING IMPLEMENTATION OF CCSS IN SCIENCE

On July 19, 2011, the "Framework for K–12 Science Education" was completed by the National Research Council (NRC). The framework clarifies the most important scientific practices, concepts, and ideas that all students should know by the time they graduate high school.

> The framework organizes science education around three dimensions:
>
> - Scientific and engineering practices. The framework identifies eight key practices that students should learn, such as asking questions and defining problems, planning and carrying out investigations, and engaging in argument from evidence.
> - Crosscutting concepts. The framework also specifies seven concepts students should learn—such as "cause and effect" and "patterns"—that have explanatory value across much of science and engineering.
> - Disciplinary core ideas. The framework identifies ideas in four disciplinary areas—life sciences; physical sciences; earth and space sciences; and engineering, technology, and the applications of science. Students' knowledge of these ideas should deepen over time, and the framework specifies aspects of each idea that students should know by the end of grades two, five, eight, and twelve.
>
> The purpose of the framework is to be the foundation for the development of new science standards. (Pietersen, 2011, p. 1)

The National Research Council framework was produced to guide the standards by providing a blueprint for them. The framework was designed to explain the ideas behind the standards, make the case for why they are needed, and explain what they hope to accomplish (Robelen, 2013b).

Such lofty and rigorous standards will need an enormous amount of buy-in both from the states and from individual teachers who will have to retool their scientific skills, knowledge, and pedagogy. Recognizing the depth and breadth of this challenge, several steps have already been taken.

The National Science Teachers Association (NSTA) has created several webinars, articles, and readers' guides to the standards and the framework. At their annual conference in April 2013, the standards were a major focus. "The group is working with Achieve and states to build a tool to guide states in ensuring that instructional units fit the standards" (Robelen, 2013a, p. 12).

The Council of State Science Supervisors held a two-day meeting in June 2013 that focused on implementation challenges. Such implementation issues as assessment, instruction, and professional development for the standards were key issues addressed.

Due to the challenging and rigorous nature of the standards, the standards demand deeper knowledge of core concepts, even though they cover less ground. Pruitt, from Achieve, believes "there is going to be a much greater level of content knowledge needed here from both the teachers and the students. . . . The reason for that is how they use the knowledge. . . . Constructing an explanation is not just saying mitosis has four phases" (as cited in Robelen, 2013a, p. 13).

Educators have expressed their own discomfort with the forthcoming standards. More than half of all elementary school teachers interviewed felt that they did not "feel very well prepared" to teach science (Robelen, 2013a, p. 13). In order to address that problem, experts in the field believe that teachers will need large-scale professional development opportunities.

Suzanne Wilson, a professor of teacher education at Michigan State University, writing for *Science*, indicated that currently professional development is a "smorgasbord of opportunities with various levels of quality and current research findings provided for attendees" (as cited in Robelen, 2013a, p. 13).

Another major challenge comes from the task of designing curriculum, instructional practices, and assessments that meet the meaning and intent of the CCSS. The integration of core principles, practices, and cross-cutting concepts poses another serious challenge for implementation.

Another area of adjustment accrues to textbook writers who will have to revamp current texts to match the forthcoming standards. Nothing is NGSS-ready at this time, and textbook writers too will have to wait to see what changes happen as policy moves from formation to implementation.

LEVELS OF QUESTIONS

According to Robert Marzano (2013), "Questioning is a potentially powerful tool that teachers can use to help students better understand academic content" (p. 76). Marzano observed and worked with many teachers and organized the types of questions they ask students into four levels, each one demands students to engage in more rigorous thinking.

Level 1 Details

Level 1 questions deal with declarative knowledge. These questions ask students to recall, recognize, or retell specific details of information. Such a question might be "Describe some important characteristics of the Appalachian Trail." Although these questions are frequently thought of as lower level, they are essential to prior knowledge if students are to progress to more abstract content.

"Rigorous text-dependent questions require students to demonstrate that they not only can follow the details of what is explicitly stated but also are able to make valid claims that square with all the evidence in the text" (Coleman & Pimentel, 2012, p. 6). Therefore, even declarative-level questions can require students to use higher-order thinking skills.

Effective questions at Level 1 can engage students to pay attention to the particular ideas, dimensions, and specifics that fill each text. Science requires a close reading of all the information provided. "In science it is attention to detail that keeps readers alert to important information" (Porton, 2013, p. 130).

Level 1 questions are essential for at-risk learners, since they must begin with concrete information before abstract reasoning can occur. In addition, many discouraged learners lack the fundamental knowledge base that their non-disabled peers have obtained by the time they enter high school. High absenteeism, distracted behaviors, and lack of an internal locus of control leave many at-risk learners with what has been called "an accumulated deficit of learning."

Level 2 Characteristics

Level 2 questions ask students to describe the characteristics of a specific category. Students need to have accurate Level 1 data in order to draw valid comparisons and contrasts, and to make classifications. For example, instead of just inquiring about the characteristics of the Appalachian Trail, a Level 2 question would ask "What are some of the differences between the Appalachian Trail and the Buckeye Trail in Ohio?"

Level 2 questions require more cognitive skills than those of Level 1, but unless Level 1 information is accurate, the students will not be able to provide useful information to Level 2 questions. Level 2 questions move students' thinking from the specific details to a more general level of comprehension.

In order to be successful in science, students must be able to analyze the structure of the relationships among important concepts in a text and see the relationships among key terms. Vocabulary acquisition is, of course, vital to students' success at this level of questioning.

At Level 2, good questions should help students see something valuable that would have been missed at a more cursory reading. The relationships between key terms and concepts require focused, reflective reading and thinking. Strong Level 2 questions develop students' skills at reading in science.

Level 3 Elaborations

"Level 3 questions ask students to elaborate on the characteristics of and elements within a category. Typically, such questions require students to explain the reasons something happens. . . . Level 3 questions also require students to explain the effect of something" (Marzano, 2013, pp. 76–77).

Level 3 questions require students to examine the dynamics of why or how things occur, for example, "Which of these had the least to the greatest impact on the development of the Appalachian Trail? (1) Settlement routes (2) Indian routes (3) Mail and passenger routes (4) Gaps and passes."

Level 4 Evidence

Level 4 questions require students to provide support or appropriate evidence for their findings. A teacher might ask, "How do you know which had the greatest influence on the development of the Appalachian Trail? Cite your sources."

Students might also be asked to analyze their own thinking and use credible evidence to support their conclusions. These types of questions require time and may be the framework for longer-term projects.

"In all of the science standards, students are expected to assess the reasoning of claims made, look for supporting evidence, and evaluate the author's recommendation for solving a scientific problem" (Porton, 2013, p. 130). Students need to recognize when the author's findings support or refute the findings from other sources (Common Core State Standards Initiative, 2012).

Level 4 questions help students to evaluate information, sources, and hypotheses using a valid and reliable system for organizing, and to determine the value of information provided in a text. Questions that require supporting valid information and inferences from the text lead to mastery at this level. Questions that ask students to create an argument and present it verbally or in writing also lead to subject mastery.

How to Plan for the Levels of Questions

First teachers need to determine the specific knowledge each student must have access to in order to move through the levels of questions. Once students have gained mastery over the declarative knowledge involved, teachers must explain how the specific topic sits inside a larger category and help students understand the characteristics of the larger category. All students must demonstrate mastery of both Level 1 and Level 2 questions.

Next, teachers might want to use cooperative learning groups to tackle Level 3 questions since the literature is very clear about the benefits of cooperative learning when teaching higher-order thinking skills. Each team must provide explanations for complex relationships that will be evaluated by the entire class. This system provides the scaffolding needed for Level 4 questions.

There are three distinct tasks available for Level 4 questions. Students may be asked to cite specific sources for their explanations, examine the logic of their own reasoning, or qualify their own conclusions (Marzano, 2013). Depending on the task chosen, teachers must develop Level 4 questions that will help students reach the intended goal.

WRITING IN SCIENCE

When students are asked to respond in writing to any question in science, they are expected to provide reasonable claims, evidence that is relevant and convincing, and support from the data to confirm their conclusions. Writing in science is either informative or persuasive.

The CCSS requires students to demonstrate that they can analyze and synthesize information and present careful analysis, thoughtful claims based on the data, and clearly written findings. Standard 9, specifically, demands that students must draw evidence from a text or texts to support analysis, reflection, or research.

According to the National Assessment of Educational Progress, while students are in high school, they should spend 40 percent of their time writing arguments and 40 percent of their time writing to inform or explain (Coleman & Pimentel, 2012). Science writing gives students ample opportunities to write convincing arguments or explain complex concepts to others.

The CCSS in science has been carefully designed to focus on the "characteristics of good writing, including drawing sufficient evidence from texts, writing coherently with well-developed ideas, and writing clearly with sufficient command of standard English" (Coleman & Pimentel, 2012, p. 12).

However, all of this requires sophisticated writing skills, and at-risk students will need a great deal of scaffolding to meet these challenges.

Grant and Fisher (as cited in Porton, 2013) suggest using a variety of sentence starters to help students analyze data and frame their thinking. Such starters include, but are not limited to, the following:

My data show that over time______________________________
The evidence for this is__________________________________
Based on the data, I conclude that__________________________

There are other organizational strategies that can help struggling learners organize their thinking. The following are also suggested:

1. What are my questions?
2. What did I do?
3. What did I see?
4. What can I claim?
5. How do I know my claims are legitimate?
6. How do my ideas compare with others?
7. How have my ideas changed?

POINTS TO PONDER

In this chapter, the case has been made that it will be a while before the science standards are implemented. Such issues as the need for widespread and effective professional activities, assessments planned for science, and retooling teaching and curriculum writing require time and energy.

Marzano's (2013) four levels of questions can help teachers to frame their questions to lead students from the concrete to the abstract, all the while requiring mastery of accurate information from the students. When teachers frame their classroom strategies and formal and informal assessments using this paradigm, even at-risk students will be able to comprehend the challenging materials they will be faced with in science.

Finally, writing in science entails careful use of information and the development of credible claims that are supported by sound data. Conclusions presented must fit the data and demonstrate students' ability to analyze and synthesize. These are all challenging tasks, and some strategies for providing scaffolding have been provided.

REFLECTIONS

Even though it will be a while before the science standards are ready for implementation, understanding the relationships among the NRC, NGSS, and CCSS in science is important. By yourself or with a partner, respond to these reflection questions:

1. What is the fundamental relationship between CCSS and
   a. NRC?
   b. NGSS?
2. What are the most important features of the CCSS in science? How do they differ from current practice?
3. Why do teachers need to know the backstory of the development of the CCSS in science? How will it be useful when it is time for implementation?
4. Discuss two strategies for providing scaffolding to at-risk students in science.
5. How will teaching writing in science differ from the other content areas?

REFERENCES

Coleman, D., & Pimentel, S. (2012). Revised publishers' criteria for the Common Core State Standards in English language arts and literacy, grades 3–12.

Common Core State Standards Initiative (2012). www.corestandards.org.

Marzano, R. J. (2013). Asking questions—at four different levels. *Educational Leadership, 70* (February): 76–78.

MRey. (2011). http://blogs.edusd.net/ccss/2011/08/31/new-national-science framework-completed.

Porton, H. D. (2013). *Teaching the Standards: How to blend common core state standards into secondary instruction*. Lanham, MD: Rowman & Littlefield.

Robelen, E. W. (2013a). Common Science Standards face capacity issues. *Education Week, 15*(31), 1–12.

Robelen, E. W. (2013b). Teachers shift instructional approaches to bring "next generation" into class. *Education Week*, *32*(32), 1–18.

ADDITIONAL REFERENCES

Baird, J. R., Fensham, P. J., Gunstone, R. T., & White, R. T. (2006). The importance of reflection in improving science teaching and learning. *Journal of Research in Science Teaching, 28*(2), 163–182.

Crawford, J. (2012). Aligning your curriculum to the Common Core State Standards. Thousand Oaks, CA: Corwin.

David, L. (2012). 5 things every teacher should be doing to meet the Common Core State Standards. *Eye on Education.* www.eyeoneducation.com.

Dunkle, C. A. (2012). Leading the Common Core State Standards. Thousand Oaks, CA: Corwin.

Forty-Nine States and Territories Join Common Core State Standards Initiative (2009). www.nga.org/cms/home/news-room/news-releases/page_2009/col2-content/main.

Foster, V. A., & McAdams, C. R. (2009). A framework for creating a climate of transparency for professional performance assessment: Fostering student investment in gatekeeping. *Counselor Education and Supervision, 48*(4), 271–284.

Jago, C. (2011). *With rigor for all: Meeting Common Core Standards for reading literature* (2nd ed.). Portsmouth, NH: Heinemann.

McNulty, R. J., & Gloecker, L. C. (2011). Fewer, clearer, higher Common Core State Standards: Implications for students receiving special education services. *International Center for Leadership in Education* (February).

McTighe, J., & Wiggins, G. (2013). *Essential questions: Opening doors to student understanding.* Alexandria, VA: ASCD.